The Means of
GRACE

The Means of
GRACE

Traditioned Practice in Today's World

ANDREW C. THOMPSON

Printed in the United States of America

Paperback ISBN: 978-1-62824-227-0
Mobi ISBN: 978-1-62824-228-7
ePub ISBN: 978-1-62824-229-4
uPDF ISBN: 978-1-62824-230-0

Library of Congress Control Number: 2015948988

Cover design by Nikabrik Design
Page design by PerfecType

SEEDBED PUBLISHING
Franklin, Tennessee
Seedbed.com
SOW FOR A GREAT AWAKENING

For Mom and Dad

Contents

Part I
What We Learn from Christ:
The Instituted Means of Grace

Part II
What We Learn from Our Context:
The Prudential Means of Grace

Part III
What We Learn by Contemplation:
The General Means of Grace

Preface

I'M GRATEFUL FOR THE CONTRIBUTIONS OF OTHER
pastors and teachers before me who have written in the area
this book covers. They have taught me a great deal. These
Wesleyan authors have contributed to a revived interest
in spiritual practices and disciplines in our tradition—
helping the church to understand how a distinctly patterned
approach to discipleship lies at the heart of the Wesleyan
understanding about how transformation occurs over
time. Steve Harper and Hal Knight have written important popular-level works on Wesleyan spirituality and the
means of grace. Their contributions have been important
in retrieving the language of the means of grace for a broad
Wesleyan audience. I've been particularly influenced by
Knight's academic-level work on the means of grace as
well. Other contributions by Dean Blevins, Ole Borgen,
Kenneth Collins, Richard Heitzenrater, and Randy Maddox
have also been deeply influential on both my thinking and
practice of the means of grace.

My reason for writing this book is threefold. First, I
want to show the deep connection between biblical spirituality and practical discipleship. John Wesley believed
that the means of grace are important primarily because
together they are the pattern of faithful discipleship we find
given to us in the Bible. Wesley taught that the means of
grace are given to us by Jesus Christ in the four gospels

of Matthew, Mark, Luke, and John. They are also the way the early church patterned its life in the Acts of the Apostles. So in a way, the entire Wesleyan teaching around the means of grace is a way to try and explain the biblical model of discipleship for the Christian life. I find that part of Wesley's practical theology to be utterly compelling and I believe it should be shared far and wide.

Second, I wanted to write this book to share with a broad audience the actual structure and approach that Wesley used in applying the means of grace to practical life. We live in such a consumerist culture that we apply that mind-set to everything we do—including our practice of discipleship. I've met Christians who talk about how they love to study the Bible or find their primary connection to God in prayer. Others will say that they practice their discipleship through their participation in service projects or mission trips. Still others think of their practice of faith as focused primarily in Sunday morning worship. The reality about the Wesleyan approach to discipleship is that there is no buffet-style picking and choosing. Instead, there is a strong conviction that the means of grace should serve as the "pattern of the Christian life" (to use Knight's phrase). Only when we live into a form of discipleship that embraces all the means of grace do we discover ourselves growing into the kind of spiritual maturity that is spoken about in Ephesians 4:15: "we are to grow up in every way into him who is the head, into Christ."

Finally, I thought it was important to write this book as a way to offer Christians an accessible guide to practicing the means of grace in their own lives and in their own communities. We are creatures of habit, and we live our lives by routines. Sometimes we self-consciously choose those routines, and sometimes we find them imposed on us by outside circumstances. It is easy to fall into bad routines unless we make a sustained effort to do otherwise. The means of grace offer us such a choice, whereby we can embrace a holy routine that aims at forming us into real disciples of Jesus Christ. In the Wesleyan tradition, we consider the life of discipleship to point us toward nothing less than salvation in this present life—and to offer us a foretaste of the salvation that is to come.

A project of this sort would not be possible without a wonderful group of people who have offered their support and encouragement along the way. J. D. Walt and Andrew Miller at Seedbed Publishing were encouraging of this book from the beginning; Andrew, in particular, has been a conversation partner throughout the writing process and has been gracious with both feedback and deadline extensions. The whole Seedbed team is a joy to work with.

Some of the content in this book served first as teaching topics in church and seminary settings. I'm grateful to the congregations of Mt. Carmel United Methodist Church (Henderson, NC), Duke's Chapel United Methodist Church (Durham, NC), and Marion United Methodist Church (Marion, AR), for their willingness to engage material on the means of grace through sermons and other teaching sessions. I am especially indebted to the students in my "Means of Grace in the Wesleyan Tradition" course at Memphis Theological Seminary, in both the fall of 2012 and the spring of 2015, for the lively conversations we had and the insights they provided.

My greatest thanks go to my wife, Emily, and our three children: Alice, Stuart, and Anna Charlotte. They are patient with me beyond anything I have a right to expect, and they indulge my tendency to lose myself down one theological rabbit hole after another. Alice, at age four, shows promise of becoming the theologian I could never hope to be. To God alone be the glory, for them and for the opportunity to write this book while living with and loving them.

Finally, I want to offer my love and gratitude to my parents, Charlotte and Robert Thompson. In ways beyond counting they gave me the kind of upbringing that helped me to know the power of the means of grace before I ever learned the term itself. Both the life of our family and the life of the church to which our family belonged provided me with my earliest spiritual formation and encounter with the grace we find in Jesus Christ. Not long after my first daughter was born, my mom said to me in an almost offhand way, "Andrew, now you'll know how I've felt about you for all these years." Those were true words. Also true is the fact that we often fail to express our deepest sentiments toward those we love in an adequate way. I have no words to tell Mom and Dad fully how I feel about them, but I do have this book. And so I dedicate it to them.

Looking for Direction

DISCIPLESHIP.

That's the word I've heard all my life to describe what the Christian faith is supposed to be about. What do you call people who follow Jesus Christ? *Disciples*. What is the word we use for the stuff Jesus' followers do in service to him? *Discipleship*. Disciple is a biblical term as well. Jesus' closest companions in the Gospels are called the twelve disciples. And in the Great Commission at the end of the Gospel of Matthew, Jesus commands his followers to go into the world and "make disciples of all nations."

So the Bible tells us that Jesus' followers are called disciples. If we want to be counted among those followers, then doesn't it make sense that we figure out just what is a disciple?

A Personal Story

My trouble for the longest time when I was a kid was that I didn't know what discipleship was supposed to look like. Was it just going to church regularly? Saying your prayers at night? Was it being involved in a certain kind of activity or service work? Being a nice person? One problem with identifying what discipleship looked like in practical life was that nobody ever really told me. My family was always active in our church when I was growing up. I went to Sunday school and attended worship every week. I learned stories from the Bible and heard sermons about God's love. I also remember being taught about faith—which was believing that Jesus Christ is the Son of God and Savior of the world.

But discipleship? I'm not sure we ever went in-depth on that.

I think I also did what a lot of other kids did, which was to think about church or faith as one thing in my life among many other things. Sure, church was important. But so were family, school, sports, playing with friends, and so on. I never really got around to *integrating* my faith into every other part of my life. Church had its place, but it was pretty neatly parceled out to certain days of the week and certain regular events. When I was there, I gave my mind and heart over to it. But when I was elsewhere, my mind and heart were occupied with other things.

When I left home at age eighteen, I left all the structure that life had provided me up to that point. All of a sudden, the strongest positive influences in my life (especially my parents) were hours away. Pretty soon I lost any sense of grounding as to what I was doing and why. My faith in Jesus Christ waned and my connection to his church soon fell by the wayside. I drifted with the wind—for years, actually. Like a lot of people at that age, I dove headlong into habits that were not healthy for my mind, body, or spirit.

Looking back, I think I was waiting for a monumental change from childhood to adulthood to happen, as if I would change from a caterpillar to a butterfly. Instead all I found was that the same old longings and fears I had always had were still there. If anything, they had become deeper (and I became more and more unsatisfied). A hunger gnawed at me, and none of the ways I tried to satisfy it worked. Typically they only made things worse. I tried to fill my hunger with new experiences, new relationships, and new adventures. What I didn't understand was that my hunger was a spiritual hunger.

By the time I was in my early twenties, I was miserable. So finally I started to pray again, almost as a last resort. (Not because I had much confidence in my prayers, but because nothing else in my life had seemed to work.) My grandfather's death had a huge impact on me around that time. In fact, I felt the first hints of a kind of inward renewal when my prayers following his death seemed like they were answered. I even began to go to church again after years of staying away—hesitantly at first, but later with real energy for a recommitment to my faith. At some point I realized that Jesus had never left me; I had only left him. My heart began to open after a long time of being closed, and I felt as if a part of me that had died was being made to live again.

During this period of renewal in my life, I was digging into the Christian faith in ways I never had. I was reading books and having conversations and embracing devotional practices that were really meeting the spiritual hunger I had so long misunderstood. But surprisingly, this new direction in my life was increasing my inward hunger at the same time! I was still taking baby steps, but I was also starting to realize that there were some things I needed if I wanted to really gain traction and grow spiritually. The main thing that I needed, I finally realized, was a pattern or framework for . . . well, *discipleship* of course. I needed to learn what the life of a real disciple of Jesus looked like.

The Way of Discipleship vs. The Way of the World

In the years that followed, I sought to find out about discipleship through a combination of study and practice. I began reading the Bible seriously for the first time in my life. I also started reading a lot of John Wesley's writings—the founder of the Methodist movement in the eighteenth century who wrote a great deal on grace, salvation, and the Christian life. In many ways, Wesley became a spiritual mentor to me. His writings helped me understand the biblical witness much more clearly.

Together with my studies, I began to take the practice of my discipleship more seriously. I came to the realization that discipleship wasn't just about "doing the right thing" out of a sense of duty or obligation. Instead it was about loving the Lord my God and loving my neighbor. If I got those things right, then all the activity of day-to-day life would follow. I was fortunate at this time to have mentors and friends much wiser than I who showed me the right path again and again. They were God's instruments in my life.

Eventually I became convinced that three things were absolutely essential for real discipleship. They are discipleship's three necessary ingredients, you might say. Without all three of them, you will end up with something that might resemble discipleship in a surface way but in reality is something quite different. Those three components are:

1. Community
2. Discipline
3. Transformation

The right kind of *community* is essential for true discipleship because none of us can go it alone. There's a reason that Jesus called twelve disciples together instead of just one. There's also a reason that the church stuck together as a community after Jesus' resurrection rather than splitting up. Without a community around you to teach you, support you, and hold you accountable, you will never grow to be a mature disciple.

We also need *discipline* in order to become real disciples of Jesus. For the same reason that an athlete will never achieve excellence without dedication and practice, we will never become the kind of disciples God wants us to be without those same things. It took me a while to come around to this understanding. I knew it was true for sports, just as I knew it was true for academics and business. But I never applied the same standard to my

> "The soul and body make a man, and the spirit and discipline make a Christian."
> —John Wesley[1]

faith. When I began to realize that my faith was the most important part of my life, then I also saw how much I had missed by approaching it in a lackadaisical and haphazard fashion.

The last thing we must have for true discipleship is the experience of *transformation*. This one is a little tricky, because *we* can't make it happen. We don't transform ourselves. Rather, we experience transformation by God's grace. Yet the very way that God's grace works means that we can expect to be transformed as we commit ourselves to the practice of discipleship within a community of faith. In other words, God promises us that we will be transformed when we live faithful lives over time.

I really think that these three elements—community, discipline, and transformation—are very countercultural today. They make up what I would call the "way of discipleship." Our culture gives us a different pattern for how to live. We will call it the "way of the world." Where God calls us to be a part of a community, the culture promotes individualism at every turn. Likewise, where true discipleship calls for true discipline, our culture encourages rabid consumerism (which means nothing more than saying "yes" to every felt desire we have). And where the gospel promises transformation, our culture promotes a kind of materialism that says we should not put our faith in God but rather in the things of this world.

I spent long enough embracing the way of the world that I came to realize how empty it is in the end. I am still very much a disciple-in-training. There is plenty that I don't do well, and there's plenty else that I still have to learn. I need all the help I can get! But I am convinced that the only life worth living is a life following Jesus Christ. It's in that kind of life that the only true happiness can be found.

The Pattern of Christian Discipleship

John Wesley had a phrase for what it means to live faithfully as a disciple of Jesus: *walking in the ways of God.* I love that phrase because it makes me think of discipleship as an action verb. It means that discipleship is really about how you live every day of your life. It's about taking seriously those things that are of greatest value, and making them your top priority.[2]

There is actually a Wesleyan pattern of discipleship for how to understand what these ways of God are. It's a pattern that shows us how to build up holy habits in our daily lives. One of the interesting things you'll find when you read the work of neuroscientists and psychologists who study human behavior is that we are all very much creatures of habit.[3] Even without meaning to do so, we will form habits that guide our day-to-day behavior. Once established, habits are very difficult to break. So that means that establishing the right kind of habits is really important.

When we talk about discipleship having a pattern, we mean that there are *faith habits* that work together to mold us into mature Christians. These faith habits are the subject of this book. They're called the "means of grace."

John Wesley and the early Methodist movement have had a profound impact on how I think about discipleship. The practices that we call the means of grace are all drawn from biblical examples, but it is through John Wesley's writings and the example of the early Methodists that we find the means of grace put together into a framework that offers us a real pattern of discipleship.[4] When I teach Wesleyan theology, I always tell my students that we should only ever read John Wesley (or any Christian theologian) insofar as he gives us a clear window into Scripture. I believe Wesley does give us such a window, and that's why I've taken his views on the means of grace seriously. It's also why I want to share this part of Wesley's approach to discipleship with you.

In the chapters that follow, you will read about what the means of grace are. You will also read about how they can work together to shape your very life. I'll warn you on the front end: the means of grace call for dedication both to a faith community and to a life of discipline. If you don't want those things as a part of your life, you might want to stop reading now. But if you have a sense that both a real community and real discipline do lie at the heart of a mature faith, then I can tell you that the means of grace *will* lead to transformation for you. I say that not because I promise it but because I believe that God promises it.

Nothing about discipleship is possible apart from God's grace. Because of that, the first chapter to follow this introduction will be about grace. *Grace* is a word that is used repeatedly throughout the New Testament, but it is not always well understood. Chapter 1 will present grace in a way that will help you to understand how important it is and how powerful it is. This chapter will also describe just what we mean by "the means of grace."

The chapters that follow after that (chapters 2–10) will be divided into three parts:

- instituted means of grace (chapters 2–7);
- prudential means of grace (chapters 8–9); and
- general means of grace (chapter 10).

These are categories that John Wesley used to help explain how the means of grace work in the Christian life. Don't get intimidated by the terms. They will make more sense as you read on.

You'll find that all the chapters on the instituted means of grace will follow the same approach. Because these are the means of grace most obviously identifiable from the life of Jesus, the way we can talk about them is pretty standard. The first section of each of the chapters will explain the biblical witness on that particular area. The second section will discuss where we find each means of grace within the history of Wesleyan spirituality. The third section will look at how to think about the topics in practical life.

The remaining chapters on the prudential and general means of grace are arranged a little bit differently, mostly because how we identify them is based on a combination of the Bible and our own experiences. But with them, I also try to stay focused on both the way a Wesleyan view on them helps us to understand them better and how we can apply them in daily life. My hope throughout is that you'll see how each one of these wonderful practices of discipleship is grounded in the Bible, given shape through the Wesleyan witness, and applicable in daily life. They are the channels that have been given to us so that we can learn how to walk in the ways of God!

The Means of
GRACE

CHAPTER 1

What Does Grace Have to Do with Me?

WHAT DO YOU KNOW ABOUT GRACE? IT'S A WORD that shows up a lot in the Bible. You've probably come across the phrase, "For by grace you have been saved through faith." That comes from Ephesians 2:8, and many Christians see it as lying at the heart of their faith.

A favorite passage of mine comes from the Gospel of John: "The Word became flesh and dwelt among us, and we have seen his glory, glory as of the only Son from the Father, full of grace and truth. . . . And from his fullness we have all received, grace upon grace" (John 1:14, 16). Those two verses say something important about how much God loves us. He loves us so much that he came into the world in the person of Jesus Christ to save us. But notice also how that great act of God is described. The Son is full of *grace* and truth. He has given us something described as *grace upon grace*.

If you think about what these biblical passages from Ephesians and John are saying, then it becomes pretty obvious that grace is important. You might even say that our salvation depends on it! So what exactly *is* grace?

3

Grace: Pardon and Power

I teach regularly about grace in churches and seminary classrooms. Regardless of the setting, I always begin by asking people what words come to mind when they think about the meaning of grace. The responses I get most often look like this: *forgiveness*, *pardon*, *mercy*, and *unmerited favor*. Those are all important terms that say something about what grace is. In the Bible, the meaning of grace might be best captured by the First Letter of John: "This is how we know what love is: Jesus Christ laid down his life for us" (1 John 3:16 NIV).

If we want to know *why* Jesus Christ laying down his life for us is the one thing that shows us love in its purest form, then we'll have to explore the Bible's story of our relationship with God more deeply. But for a one-sentence statement about what God's love is about, I'll take that one from 1 John 3:16.

Wait—did you notice what I just did? I switched from talking about God's grace to talking about God's love. That happens quite a bit when we get into the biblical language about what grace is. Grace is really a word to describe how God is *for us* in every way. So it makes sense to talk about grace in terms of God's love, because it is through God's love that we find ourselves forgiven. We know grace when we receive pardon for our sin. Grace is pardon.

There's another way to speak about grace as well. If forgiveness for sin is one part of what grace is, then the second way to understand grace is that it is God's power for new life. In his second letter, Peter counsels us to "grow in the grace and knowledge of our Lord and Savior Jesus

Christ" (2 Peter 3:18). He's talking about grace as a kind of power that allows us to grow spiritually so that we come to know Christ more fully.

The apostle Paul also talks about grace as a type of divine power. He says in Ephesians 4:7 that "to each one of us grace has been given as Christ apportioned it" (NIV). And the reason for giving this grace is to raise up mature leaders in the church, "to prepare God's people for works of service"

> "What is Grace? The Power of the Holy Ghost, enabling us to believe and love and serve God."
> —John Wesley[1]

(Eph. 4:12 NIV). Once again, we see grace being described as a kind of power for the life of discipleship.

You may have experienced grace in both of these ways. As a child, you knew when you did something wrong that things weren't going to feel right again until your mom or dad forgave you. While the context might change as you grow older, the need to be reconciled when something goes awry doesn't change. Whether it is a friend, your husband or wife, or a coworker, you know that you need to be forgiven when you've messed up in some way. Sometimes, of course, you are the one who needs to do the forgiving!

Christians who have received new birth in Christ can often speak profoundly about the sense of being forgiven by God. When grace is given and truly received in faith, then the sense of all the burden of past sin and broken relationships is lifted. Pardon for sin—the forgiveness that can only be found in Christ Jesus—is experienced through grace in its purest form.

What about experiencing not just the pardon but also the power of grace? The way we encounter the power of God's grace is not likely to be as momentary and sudden as it is in that first wonderful experience of forgiveness. The power of grace is most likely to be experienced as the gentle but persistent force that nurtures our growth as disciples of Jesus. In fact, John Wesley often considered grace to be just that—the power of the Holy Spirit at work within us to help us grow spiritually.[2] It is true that the Holy Spirit can work dramatically at certain points in our lives. On a day-to-day basis, though, the Spirit's work is going to be subtler than that and nourishing to us in ways we might not always even realize. Like the effects of good sunlight, healthy soil, and ample water in a garden, the grace given through the Holy Spirit gives us what we need to grow just the right way so that we eventually bear wonderful fruit.

What's the Big Deal about Grace?

So far I've talked a lot about how we can understand grace as it's shown to us in the Bible. But there are a couple of questions you might be asking at this point. Why do we need to be forgiven in the first place? And what kind of power does grace give me to grow that I don't have just by living in the world?

These are good questions to ask. For some people, the answers are obvious. For others, they aren't obvious at all. The need for both pardon and power from God are due to what the Bible calls "sin." But since a word like sin isn't really self-explanatory, it is worth looking at how the Bible describes it. Let me do that here.

There are really two ways we can think about sin: it is both an act and a disease. The notion of sinful acts is the easier of the two for us to wrap our minds around. We're all taught from a young age that there are things we aren't supposed to do. *Don't hit your sister. Stop grabbing toys away from the other children. Don't take an extra cookie from the cookie jar.* Those are all household rules, which are established by moms and dads to teach kids right from wrong. When we grow older, we learn that there are laws that our towns and cities and states have put into place to make sure society is livable. *Obey the speed limit. Don't steal other people's things. Pay your taxes each year.* So young or old, we're confronted with a world where there are certain rules or laws we're expected to keep in obedience to the authority over us (our parents, the government). Those authorities are responsible for keeping the peace and providing a good environment in which to live. Rules are necessary for that.

The Bible teaches us that God is the creator of all things, including us. God also loves everything that he has made, which we see in a passage from Psalm 145:9 that was one of John Wesley's favorites: "The LORD is good to all: and his tender mercies are over all his works" (KJV). So beyond being just the creator, God is the governor of creation as well. As governor, God has also seen the need to establish a law for his creation and especially for those special creatures that he has made in his own image—human beings. One place we see God's law summarized is in the Ten Commandments:

The Ten Commandments

(Loving God)	(Loving Neighbor)
1. You shall have no other gods before God	5. Honor your father and mother
2. You shall not cast idols	6. You shall not murder
3. You shall not take the name of God in vain	7. You shall not commit adultery
4. You shall honor the Sabbath and keep it holy	8. You shall not steal
	9. You shall not bear false witness
	10. You shall not covet

God's law does more than constrain wrongdoing (although it does do that). It also shows us how to embrace all that is good. As you can see in the previous diagram, the Ten Commandments give us guidance about how to love God and how to love our neighbor.

Sin comes into the picture when we break God's law. We can do this through outward acts and we can also commit acts of the heart when we sin through our thoughts and desires. "Create in me a clean heart, O God," Psalm 51:10 says, "and renew a right spirit within me." It is a statement that recognizes the way that outwardly sinful acts usually begin as sins of the heart.

Sin is like a disease inside us as well. This may not be quite as obvious, but it explains everything about why we end up committing sinful acts at all—especially when we know such acts are wrong. Sin is like a plague that everyone in the human race is born with. The apostle Paul spoke about this in his personal testimony when he said that sin "deceived me" and "killed me" and that he had been "sold under sin." For Paul, sin was like a presence that was constantly pressing him to do evil rather than good: "I do not understand my own actions. For I do not do what I want, but I do the very thing I hate" (Rom. 7:15).

When we think about sin not just as things we do but as a presence within us, we begin to understand just what a problem it is. You can't just decide that, starting right now, you're not going to sin anymore. It just isn't that simple! What's worse, sin is something that affects the whole human race. Paul told us that "all have sinned and fall short of the glory of God" (Rom. 3:23). That means that there isn't anyone who is free from the predicament of sin. We are alienated from God, living broken lives in a broken world. Whether it is in our actions or our hearts, we are constantly living lives of rebellion against the One who created us and will ultimately judge us.

Grace at Work

That word—*judge*—can be a scary one. But it is another one of those terms we use to describe how God relates to us: Creator, Governor, and Judge. We do stand on the outside of God's law because of our sin. As our judge, God should be expected to hold us accountable for our rebellion against the good and holy plan he has for our lives.

It's here that we can come full circle to where we began, though. We started by talking about God's grace. When we talk about grace as God's love for us, the pardon and power of God in our lives, it all sounds great. But it's only when we come to grips with the enormity of our sin that we truly realize why grace is necessary. Otherwise we might look at grace in a take-it-or-leave-it fashion. The truth, of course, is that we stand in desperate need of God's grace in every possible way.

Once we understand our deep need for grace, how can we understand the way that grace actually works in our lives? After all, saying that grace is God's love for us is one thing. Understanding how we receive that love is another. I can open up my arms to receive a hug from my wife or my brother. But how do I open up my arms to receive God's grace?

Not long ago I heard Bishop Gary Mueller of the United Methodist Church present a teaching on the Wesleyan view of how grace works.[3] He describes God's grace interacting with us in these three ways:

- Grace is unconditional—God comes to each of us with the message that he loves us as we are, no matter our past, etc.
- Grace is transformational—God does not leave us as we are but rather transforms our hearts and lives.
- Grace is invitational—By grace, the Lord Jesus calls and empowers us to join him in the work of the gospel.

This is a wonderful way to capture the Wesleyan sense of how grace works in our lives. *Unconditional, transformational*, and *invitational*—these are terms that speak to the way the Bible shows how grace works, and they also help us to think about how the Wesleyan approach takes the biblical view seriously as it relates to daily discipleship.

Grace Is Unconditional

I have a friend named Katherine who is a potter. We worked together for several summers in a program for high school youth. Katherine uses her skill in pottery to teach biblical lessons. Sitting at her potter's wheel with her arms covered in clay, she shares stories of how God molds us like a master potter. She knows her source: the Bible speaks about God in this way. Jeremiah 18:6 says, "Just like clay in the potter's hand, so are you in my hand, O house of Israel" (NRSV). For my friend Katherine, the image of God as the potter and us as the clay speaks to the loving care that God has for the whole creation.

When we talk about God's grace as unconditional, we mean that God loves absolutely everything he has made. The potter does not take up the clay, mold it, and work it if he hates the clay to begin with. And that is true of God in relation to the world. God is the master potter, and we are the work of his hands. God loves us.

When we talk about grace as unconditional, what we also mean by that is that there's nothing we have to do in order to *earn* God's love. And considering how limited we are and how infinite God is, that's a very good thing! The unconditional nature of grace also means that there is no one that God excludes from his mercy. As it has often been said, this doesn't mean that all people *will* be saved but it does mean that all people *can* be saved. This universal, unconditional offer of grace is attested to throughout the Bible. The entire thrust of the New Testament message about Jesus Christ is based on this—that he came as "the atoning sacrifice for our sins, and not for ours only but also for the sins of the whole world" (1 John 2:2 NRSV).

Grace Is Transformational

At its heart, grace is about growth. It is about taking us from where we are to where God wants us to be. This part of how grace affects us is summed up for me in two simple sentences:

1. Jesus Christ loves you just the way you are.
2. Jesus Christ loves you so much that he refuses to leave you the way you are.

Saying that Jesus loves us just as we are is important—it's what allows us to speak about the unconditional nature of grace in the first place. But when we go on to say that Jesus' love for us is so great that he wants to change us in some way, we are getting at the heart of the move from sin to salvation. We're now speaking about the way that God's grace is deeply transformational as well.

In the Bible, the two great themes of justification and new birth are related to the transformational power of grace. *Justification* sounds like a difficult word, but its meaning is simple. It means for something that is out of alignment to be put back right again. In this case, what is out of alignment is us. We are broken creatures. Our thoughts and deeds are often marked by sin. We have a wound within us that we don't have the power to heal on our own. To be justified by God's grace means that God puts us back in alignment with him. It means to be forgiven. This comes through the atoning work of Jesus Christ on the cross, when it is received by us personally. Jesus had no sin, but he suffered for our sin nevertheless. And he did this out of the depths of his love for us.

The new birth is the powerful experience of spiritual regeneration that comes in the wake of our justification. If justification is really about how we are viewed in God's eyes, then the new birth is about how we come to be viewed in our own eyes. Peter refers to this great change when he speaks about the way that God the Father "has given us a new birth into a living hope through the resurrection of Jesus Christ from the dead" (1 Peter 1:3 NRSV). Our spiritual birth is the beginning of an ongoing growth in grace, which the Bible calls sanctification.

I know, I know. *Sanctification* sounds like another tricky term. But it's really just another word for holiness. And in the New Testament, holiness is the word used to describe what happens to us when we are brought closer and closer to the heart of God by Jesus. We are made holy by that process.

Justification =
Being made right

Sanctification =
Being made holy

I grew up as a Methodist, but I never really heard words like *sanctification* or *holiness* during my childhood. So I was surprised to find out later that this idea was probably the most central spiritual concept for John Wesley (who, after all, was the leader of the Methodist revival). He believed that the best understanding of holiness is that it is all about love. And the book of the Bible that he thought captured holy love the best was the First Letter of John. "God's love was revealed among us in this way," John told us in 1 John 4:9, "God sent his only Son into the world so that we might live through him" (NRSV). Coming to faith in Jesus Christ holds profound spiritual meaning. It creates a change in us; it makes us holy. "God is love," John explained, "and those who abide in love abide in God, and God abides in them" (1 John 4:16b NRSV).

When we say that grace is transformational, we mean that Christ does not leave us as he finds us. Just as Jesus made the lame to walk, the blind to see, and the dead to be raised, so too does Jesus seek to heal us as well. Grace has the ability to forgive us for the wrongs we have committed. Grace also has the ability to heal us from the tendency to do wrong and be wrong. Think about it: if God only forgave us but didn't heal us, then we'd end up right where we started in terms of our sin. Yet because the nature of grace is about both pardon *and* power, we can be both forgiven and healed!

The apostle Paul teaches us that the transforming power of grace works in our lives every day so long as we are continuing to walk in faith. "All of us," Paul said, "with unveiled faces, seeing the glory of the Lord as though reflected in a mirror, are being transformed into the same image from one degree of glory to another" (2 Cor. 3:18 NRSV). Walking in the ways of God is like gazing into God's own image. When we do that, we begin to be transformed into that same image. That means that life lived in the midst of God's grace is a different kind of life than we could ever live otherwise.

Grace Is Invitational

Unconditional, transformational, and . . . invitational! What does it mean to say that grace is invitational? What is God inviting us to do by the working of his grace?

One of the great examples of invitational grace channeled through a person in my lifetime happened when I was in high school. It was the spring of 1993, and the famous college basketball coach Jim Valvano was dying of cancer. He was named as the recipient of the Arthur Ashe Courage and Humanitarian Award at the first annual ESPY Awards that year. Valvano was very sick by the time the awards ceremony came around, but somehow he was able to make it there. His friend Dick Vitale had to help him up to the podium so he could receive his award.[4]

Jimmy V took the mic when it came time for him to speak and didn't give it back for eleven minutes. He spoke about his love for his family. He spoke about his enthusiasm for life. He brought just about everyone in the audience to tears. Toward the end of the speech Valvano said, "I just got one last thing, I urge all of you, all of you, to enjoy your life, the precious moments you have. To spend each day with some laughter and some thought, to get your emotions going. To be enthusiastic every day and . . . to keep your dreams alive in spite of problems, whatever you have."[5]

A powerful message. But he didn't stop there. He went on to urge the audience to join the fight against cancer and AIDS by getting involved and donating their time and energy and money. To make a difference somehow.

Then he ended by offering words of great assurance. He said that the cancer in his own body could only damage him so much. "It cannot touch my mind, it cannot touch my heart and it cannot touch my soul," Valvano said. "And those three things are going to carry on forever."

I've watched the video of Jimmy V's speech many times. I've read the text of it word-for-word. The man was talking about God and about salvation. I don't know how else to understand his closing words other than as words of great faith, spoken by someone sure of his salvation in Jesus Christ. When you couple those words with his encouragement to embrace life fully, to love boldly, and to do good works in the world, I think you have the perfect image of what the invitational work of grace is all about.

I have always found it interesting that Jesus even bothered calling fishermen and tax collectors to follow him. He was the Son of God. He surely didn't need help from people who were inevitably going to get in the way more than anything else! Yet call them he did. He spent a whole lot of time teaching them and preparing them to carry out ministries of their own. When you read the stories of the four Gospels—Matthew, Mark, Luke, and John—you can't escape the sense that a big part of what it means to be Jesus' disciple is to take the good news Jesus has given you and carry it out into the world so that others might come to know Jesus too.

He offers us his love so that we might be transformed. Then he invites us to carry that love to others so that they will be transformed as well.

The Purpose of the Means of Grace

Once we know this wonderful grace of God firsthand, we begin to want to encounter it in an ongoing way. God wants that as well. He has given us certain channels through which we can receive grace. They are the means of grace.

John Wesley called the means of grace "signs, words, or actions ordained of God" and "channels of conveying his grace to the souls of men."[6] What he really meant is that they are discipleship practices that we draw from the biblical witness. Wesley saw the life of the early church as the perfect model for how the means of grace should be located at the very heart of Christian discipleship. A key Scripture passage comes from the Acts of the Apostles, which tells us what the first Christians did following their baptism: "They devoted themselves to the apostles' teaching and the fellowship, to the breaking of bread and the prayers" (Acts 2:42). From this fertile ground of practical faith, many spiritual fruits were borne. Acts tells us that "awe came upon every soul," that they met together daily and cared for one another's material needs, and that their hearts were made glad by the rich spiritual fellowship they shared (vv. 43–46). In fact, it was through their faithful use of these means of grace that God's gift of salvation was received. The passage concludes, "And the Lord added to their number day by day those who were being saved" (v. 47).[7]

So it's no wonder that Wesley put great stock in the importance of practices like prayer, the Lord's Supper, searching the Scriptures, and robust fellowship. When he claimed that such things were ordained by God to serve as channels of grace into the lives of believers, he could point to a pretty solid biblical precedent! Since the time of the Pentecost, these are the very ways that God has been mediating his saving grace to the church.

The way that the Acts of the Apostles speaks of the means of grace as the daily practices of the Christian community also tells us something important about how they are meant to be used in the present. As practices, they are not one-time acts that supply us with all that we need in a single moment. They are also not solitary activities that we do in isolation from others. The means of grace are, most fundamentally, practices of discipleship that we embrace in an ongoing way within the community of faith. Their power is not in the practices themselves, but rather in the grace that those practices mediate through the Holy Spirit. Yet the practices are important; when they are engaged in a disciplined way, they become holy habits that work to transform us in heart and life.

Since we are human beings who undertake meaningful activities in all areas of our lives, it only makes sense that the way God would choose to convey his grace would be through day-to-day practices. Some of these practices are *instituted* in the sense that they are clearly present in both the teaching and example of Jesus Christ. (Thus, Christ has instituted them, or put them in place, directly.) Other practices are *prudential* in character, meaning that we use the biblical witness in conjunction with our practical wisdom to figure out what they look like in our own context. Still other practices are more *general* in that they are made up of more inward, contemplative disciplines that help us to stay focused on God in our daily living. I like to think of these three main categories of the means of grace in this way:

- instituted means of grace: what we learn from Christ;
- prudential means of grace: what we learn from our context; and
- general means of grace: what we learn by contemplation.

The means of grace offer us a whole pattern for the life of discipleship. When we practice them regularly and with discipline, they also lead us to understand grace more and more. And that shows us ever more deeply how much God loves us.

This is all wonderful good news, and it leads us into the heart of what this book is about. It's in our nature to follow *something*—and grace gives us the ability to turn to Jesus Christ and follow him. Now it is time to look at the kind of life that is needed in order to truly grow toward spiritual maturity. There is a pattern to discipleship, and that pattern goes by a particular term: the means of grace.

PART I

What We Learn from Christ:

The Instituted Means of Grace

"They devoted themselves to the apostles' teaching and the fellowship, to the breaking of bread and the prayers. . . . And the Lord added to their number day by day those who were being saved."

—Acts 2:42, 47

CHAPTER 2

Baptism

WATER HAS GREAT POWER. IT CAN SHOW THAT power in some pretty amazing ways. Life can't exist without water. A drought in the summer makes crops wither in the fields. Take it away from us humans for just a few days and we die. Water makes our food grow. It renews the ground. We drink it, bathe in it, and play in it.

Too little water is deadly, but so is too much. Heavy rain can erode the ground and lead to mudslides. Hurricanes and monsoons devastate communities every year. And floodwaters can overflow the banks of rivers, causing property destruction and loss of life.

I've seen water work its power in two of the world's great rivers: the Nile River in Egypt and the Mississippi River in the United States.

A few years ago I traveled with a group of people to visit Christian sites in Egypt. One afternoon our guide took us up on a bluff where we could see the Nile from a high vantage point. The view was amazing. There it was—the longest river in the world—running as far as the eye could see both north and south. The Nile wasn't as wide as I thought it would be, but what it lacked in width it more than made up in its incredible length.

The view from that bluff also showed me what the real power of the Nile is all about for the Egyptian people. Starting on each side of the riverbank and extending a ways both to the east and the west there is a strip of irrigated, lush green land. Agriculture flourishes in those irrigated strips of land. Towns and villages thrive. Beyond the strips of irrigated land, there is only bleak desert. The Nile's water does for the people who live there today what it has always done. It gives them life.

Four years after my journey to Egypt, I saw power of a different kind wielded by the largest river in North America. The Mississippi River isn't quite as long as the Nile, but it carries a lot more water. When springtime rains are heavy in the American heartland, the tributaries of the Mississippi River can swell its size to massive proportions.

The Mississippi flooded in the spring of 2011, just when my family and I were preparing to move to Memphis, Tennessee. My wife and I went on a house-hunting trip in the area that May when the river was at its highest point. We drove from downtown Memphis across the Interstate 40 bridge into Arkansas, where the river is usually a half-mile wide. That day I measured it at a full three miles from the Tennessee side to where the water finally stopped at the edge of the levee in Arkansas. I found out later that the river crested at 47.8 feet deep—a level not seen since 1937. By that point the amount of water flowing past downtown Memphis would have filled up a football field 44 feet deep in a second![1] The US Army Corps of Engineers later reported that the flood had cost $2.8 billion in damage.[2] Water gives life, but it can also cause great destruction and death.

The power of water for life and death is everywhere in our world. It's present throughout the Scriptures as well. In the beginning as God created the heavens and the earth, the Bible tells us, God's Spirit hovered over the waters and brought order to them (Gen. 1:1–2). Yet the waters of the Great Flood in Noah's day destroyed everything that didn't make it onto the ark (Gen. 6:17–22). When Moses led the Hebrews out of Egypt through the parted waters of the Red Sea, Pharaoh's army was drowned when it tried to follow (Exod. 14:21–28). And yet, not long after that Moses drew water from the rock so God's people would not die of thirst in the wilderness (Exod. 17:1–7).

> Water is life, and water is death. This is the story of the Bible. It is the story of our world. It is also the story of baptism.

Water is life, and water is death. This is story of the Bible. It is the story of our world. It is also the story of baptism.

Baptism in the Biblical Witness

There's a story that every one of the four Gospels tells us about the beginning of Jesus' ministry. Matthew, Mark, Luke, and John all emphasize one key moment to describe how Jesus' preaching, teaching, and healing in Galilee and beyond were launched. That story is the story of Jesus' baptism by his cousin John in the River Jordan.

The Gospel of Luke tells it like this: "Now when all the people were baptized, and when Jesus also had been baptized and was praying, the heavens were opened, and the Holy Spirit descended on him in bodily form, like a

dove; and a voice came from heaven, 'You are my beloved
Son; with you I am well pleased'" (Luke 3:21–22).

This is God's way of showing us that Jesus of Nazareth
is the Christ—the Messiah who has come to save Israel.
Christians have long seen in the story of Jesus' baptism
a sign of the Trinity. As the Son of God receives baptism,
the voice of the Father offers his blessing while the Spirit
descends in the form of a dove.

Jesus' baptism shows us how baptism is important for
all those who will follow him. While his own baptism is the
first time we get that message in the New Testament, it won't
be the last. The Gospel of John tells us that Jesus' disciples
baptized others as they traveled around with him (John
4:1–3). At the very end of Jesus' ministry—after his resurrection and just before he ascends into heaven—his final
instructions to his disciples are about how baptism factors
into the spread of the church. Jesus tells his followers, "All
authority in heaven and on earth has been given to me. Go
therefore and make disciples of all nations, baptizing them
in the name of the Father and of the Son and of the Holy
Spirit, teaching them to observe all that I have commanded
you. And behold, I am with you always, to the end of the
age" (Matt. 28:18–20). This passage is often called the
Great Commission because in it Jesus commissions his
disciples for the mission they have in front of them.

The spiritual meaning of baptism is what really shows
us why it deserves a place at the head of any list of the
means of grace. Baptism is the outward sign of God's salvation. We can get a clue about how important an outward
sign like that is by using a comparison from your own daily
life. Think about how you show love to another person:
a hug, a kiss, a bouquet of flowers, a birthday present, a

ring, and words like "I love you" and "I forgive you." All of these are just regular outward actions or things. But when used in the right way, they're all intended to convey a deep emotional message to another person. When a woman kisses her husband, she's *both* signaling to him that she loves him *and* she's actually conveying that love through the sign of the kiss itself.

Baptism is a sign of God's love for us in much the same way. The person—whether an infant or child, youth or adult—comes forward to receive baptism in the midst of the church. By pouring water over that person's head and saying the words, "I baptize you in the name of the Father, and of the Son, and of the Holy Spirit," the minister carries out the first step in Jesus' teaching to make new disciples through baptism. The minister is also offering baptism to the person being baptized on behalf of the whole church—and as God's gift! There's much more to come afterward, of course. True discipleship requires a lifetime of practice and growth. But baptism is the first step.

You might ask, "But why does *this* particular thing serve as a sign of God's love?" There are really two primary reasons. The apostle Paul showed us the first one when he said in Romans 6:3–4, "Do you not know that all of us who have been baptized into Christ Jesus were baptized into his death? We were buried therefore with him by baptism into death, in order that, just as Christ was raised from the dead by the glory of the Father, we too might walk in newness of life." Being underground and being underwater share this in common: you can't breathe in either place. So the symbolism of baptism is that it unites us with Jesus in his death, and thus unites us with him as well in his resurrection.

The second reason that baptism shows us a sign of God's love is its connection with the Holy Spirit. John the Baptist knew a lot about baptism, but he also knew that his own baptism was nothing compared with the baptism that Jesus would inaugurate, saying, "I baptize you with water for repentance, but he who is coming after me is mightier than I, whose sandals I am not worthy to carry. He will baptize you with the Holy Spirit and fire" (Matt. 3:11).

Have you ever considered what it means to be united with Jesus Christ through your baptism?

Jesus later explained the connection between baptism by water and baptism by the Holy Spirit in the Gospel of John. It happened when a Pharisee named Nicodemus came to Jesus at night to ask him about his teaching. Jesus first said to Nicodemus, "No one can see the kingdom of God without being born from above." When Nicodemus replied that he didn't understand, Jesus explained further. "Very truly, I tell you, no one can enter the kingdom of God without being born of water and Spirit," Jesus said, "What is born of the flesh is flesh, and what is born of the Spirit is spirit. Do not be astonished that I said to you, 'You must be born from above'" (John 3:5–7 NRSV). We are born of water when we are born from our mother's womb. Yet the water of baptism symbolizes another birth, which is our new birth by the Holy Spirit.

Think about that connection: the water of baptism, and the grace of the Holy Spirit. A sign of God's love that conveys God's love at the same time! Baptism unites us with Christ and gives us a promise of the resurrection to come, but it also shows us that God intends to save us in the present through the power of the Spirit. In his letter to Titus, the apostle Paul spoke of "the water of rebirth and renewal by the Holy Spirit" (Titus 3:5 NRSV).

Through baptism, we can be assured of the gift of the Holy Spirit—just as Jesus promised we would.

Baptism in Wesleyan Spirituality

John Wesley called baptism, "the initiatory sacrament which enters us into covenant with God."[3] That language can seem pretty technical, but all it means is that baptism is the initial act that brings us into communion with Jesus Christ. Wesley rightly called baptism a sacrament,

> "He saved us, not because of works of righteousness that we had done, but according to his mercy, . . . by the Holy Spirit . . . through Jesus Christ our Savior, so that, having been justified by his grace, we might become heirs according to the hope of eternal life.
> —Titus 3:5–7 NRSV

which it is. A *sacrament* is an act of worship that is special because it is specifically given by Christ to his followers as a way to receive him spiritually. The Wesleyan tradition has always recognized the two sacraments of baptism and the Lord's Supper (or Holy Communion). These are the sacraments that Jesus commands his followers to practice in the Gospels—"Do this in remembrance of me" at the Last Supper and "Go into the world . . . baptizing them in the name of the Father, and of the Son, and of the Holy Spirit" in the Great Commission.

Wesley once published an instructional essay on baptism that he developed from a longer work his father had written. We call it the *Treatise on Baptism*. It offers strong biblical interpretation about how Christians should understand and practice baptism in their own churches. Wesley begins it by emphasizing the importance of baptism in the Christian life, pointing to the fact that its authority comes directly from Jesus Christ, "who alone has power to institute a proper sacrament, a sign, seal, pledge, and means of grace, perpetually obligatory on all Christians."[4]

Did you notice that key phrase—means of grace?

In most of his writings on the means of grace, Wesley leaves baptism off the list. The reason is that he's mostly interested in teaching Christians how to practice their faith daily. The one thing that all the means of grace share—*except* baptism—is that they can be repeated over and over again. Actually, the whole point is to repeat them as often as possible! Baptism is the odd duck in that sense, because we only experience it once in a lifetime. So when Wesley is writing on the importance of practicing prayer or fasting (or any of the other means of grace), there's no real reason for him to include baptism. In his context, practically everyone had been baptized as an infant or small child.

Baptism was important for Wesley, though, and it should be important for Wesleyans in any age. In fact, baptism is absolutely crucial for understanding why the rest of the means of grace are important at all. Here's why: baptism is the entry point into an entire way of life. That way of life comes to be marked by all the rest of the means of grace. But it is begun—and in some sense defined—by baptism.

Wesley's *Treatise on Baptism* offers three benefits of baptism that give us a clue as to why baptism should be at the top of the list of the means of grace. His first benefit is that the waters of baptism are a sign of the washing away of original sin through Jesus Christ's atoning death on the cross. Wesley here has in mind a passage from Ephesians that speaks of how "Christ loved the church and gave himself up for her, that he might sanctify her, having cleansed her by the washing of water with the word" (5:25–26). It is God's grace alone that forgives, but the sacrament of baptism offers us the *assurance* of that forgiveness as a sign of God's mercy.

The second is that baptism is the way we enter into covenant with God through Jesus Christ. Baptism is like circumcision in the Jewish faith in that way, except that it is a spiritual circumcision. We are united to Christ through baptism, so that we are "no longer foreigners and aliens, but fellow citizens with God's people and members of God's household" (Eph. 2:19 NIV). The outward expression of this unity is through our membership in the church—we're not individual Christians but rather Christians together within the body of Christ. There's an inward unity as well that is very powerful, though, and its meaning is glimpsed in Jesus' own baptism. When Jesus was baptized in the River Jordan, it was a moment of profound communion for God the Son together with his Father and the Holy Spirit. Even so, when we are baptized, we too are ushered into a deep spiritual communion with Jesus. We are baptized *into Christ* and thereafter we live as a part of his body—the church.

The third benefit of baptism is what Wesley calls "spiritual regeneration." Here Wesley is telling us that something really *happens* at baptism. Remember how the embrace of husband and wife is an outward sign of their inward, shared love that simultaneously conveys that love between them. It's just in this way that baptism serves as an outward sign of an inward grace and a means by which that grace is received. When Paul wrote to Titus about the "water of rebirth" and connected that with the work of the Holy Spirit, it was clear that he was telling us that God is at work in the sacrament of baptism.

"In him also you were circumcised with a spiritual circumcision, by putting off the body of the flesh in the circumcision of Christ; when you were buried with him in baptism, you were also raised with him through faith in the power of God, who raised him from the dead."

—Colossians 2:11–12 NRSV

Wesley would admonish us to take care not to confuse baptism by water and baptism by the Holy Spirit. Like most people, he would certainly affirm that the two can happen simultaneously. That doesn't have to be the case, though, just as it is clearly not the case at all times in the Acts of the Apostles when the early church was beginning to grow. Wesley's counsel about the need for spiritual rebirth is uncompromising: "The question is not what you were made in baptism," he says, "but what you are now. I ask not whether you *were* born of water and the Spirit. But *are* you *now* the temple of the Holy Ghost which dwelleth in you?"[5] So baptism is certainly a means of grace that puts us in contact with the Holy Spirit, but the spiritual new birth that is so central to a living faith is something given when the Spirit wills.

Wesleyans have always affirmed that infants and small children are worthy of receiving Christian baptism. There are many biblical reasons for doing so, not the least of which is Jesus' command, "Let the little children come to me and do not hinder them, for to such belongs the kingdom of heaven" (Matt. 19:14). When Peter began to preach the gospel on the Day of Pentecost, he instructed the people there to repent and be baptized because the promise he had delivered was for them *and their children* (see Acts 2:38–39). Later in the book of Acts, we find that entire households receive baptism together: parents, children, and household servants (see Acts 16:15, 33). Baptism is meant for all people because God's grace is meant for all people.[6]

Baptism in Our Daily Discipleship

Both the Bible and the Wesleyan witness show us the meaning of baptism and how important it is. We still have a problem with actually *practicing* baptism because we're only baptized once! We can read the Bible daily, pray at every opportunity, and receive the Lord's Supper every time we worship. Once we've been baptized, though, we never receive that sacrament again. Baptism is our initiation into the Christian faith. And once we've been adopted into God's family, we never get kicked out.

So how is baptism a part of our daily discipleship at all?

A friend of mine named Fred Edie has a wonderful image for what baptism should mean to our discipleship. He says that growing in our faith is akin to "learning to swim in our baptismal waters." Baptism is the outward sign of God's claim on your life. The water that covers us at baptism is a sign of God's grace poured into us. Baptism, in other words, ushers us into a whole new life. If we think about the water of baptism as the image of God's grace, then learning to swim in those waters is nothing less than learning what it means for our lives to be lived completely immersed in the grace of God![7]

One of the great celebrations in the life of a congregation happens when a new Christian is made through the sacrament of baptism. Whether that person is a baby, a youth, or an adult, the meaning is the same: Christ Jesus welcomes a new Christian into his fellowship, and the congregation there to bear witness makes a commitment to help that person grow into full discipleship. The moment is powerful, and it involves the whole congregation renewing its own baptismal vows. So just as we welcome the newly baptized person to begin swimming in his or her baptismal waters, we are reminded that we still swim in ours too.

The covenant that Christ makes with us at our baptism never goes away. We all live out that covenant through our worship, our discipleship, and our mission as Christian people to spread the good news. Through all of this, we can come to discover that our baptism is not truly a one-time event after all. It is a whole new way of life that we were ushered into. Baptism is truly when we begin walking in the ways of God.

The final image of God's salvation in the Bible comes in Revelation, when the New Jerusalem is described. It is the picture of the church as she will be when all things are brought to completion—the bride adorned for her husband. Running through the middle of that city will be a river, which is the River of Life. After describing this beautiful scene, Scripture tells us, "Whoever is thirsty, let him come; and whoever wishes, let him take the free gift of the water of life" (Rev. 22:17 NIV).

I read that passage as a baptismal bookend to the whole New Testament. The story of Jesus begins with a river which the Son of God enters to receive his own baptism. And that story ends with another river, which all men and women are called to seek out so that they can drink and never thirst again. The waters of that river are baptismal waters, and we are invited to dive in.

CHAPTER 3

Searching the Scriptures

OUR DAUGHTER ALICE LOVES BOOKS. SHE ALWAYS has. Alice loved looking at picture books when she was barely old enough to turn the page. At first she preferred simple touch-and-feel books. Now at four years old, she likes to have my wife, Emily, and me read more complicated storybooks to her.

One of the things I've tried to do from the start has been to read Alice a lot of Bible stories. We have a big Bible storybook that has stories from Genesis to Revelation. We also have smaller books that tell individual stories, like Noah and the Ark, Jonah and the Fish, or the Parable of the Lost Sheep. One of Alice's favorites is a little storybook that tells about the birth of Jesus. She loves that one, and I've read it to her countless times.

One day when she was barely three years old, I was getting ready to take Alice to daycare on my way to work. She walked into the kitchen holding one of her baby dolls wrapped in a little blanket. "Look!" she said. "It's the baby Jesus!"

"Oh," I said, "I see."

"Yeah!" she replied. "We're gonna put him in the manger."

I smiled at her. "That's right, isn't it? Because there's no room for him in the inn." Then I went off to hunt her socks and shoes. She stayed in the kitchen, cradling the baby doll and speaking softly to it.

I got back a few minutes later and said, "Come on, Alice. Time to go."

She looked up at me sharply. "I'm *Mary*," she said. "You're *Joseph*."

"Oh! Okay," I said. "Then let's go, Mary."

I must have looked a little startled because when I picked her up she looked at me sympathetically and said, "I love you, Joseph."

"I love you too, Mary," I said.

During the ride into town, she kept calling me Joseph and herself Mary. When we got to her daycare, I asked her if she wanted to leave the baby Jesus in the car. But she wouldn't have any of it. "No," she said. "Maybe I can share Jesus with my friends, and then when they're done they can give him back to me."

After I dropped Alice off, my mind was racing and my heart was full. I walked back out to my car amazed that she was already internalizing the biblical story enough to bring it into her play-acting.

Since that day I've thought a lot about what it means to "search the Scriptures." That's a phrase from the Gospel of John. Jesus uses it to tell his audience that they should looked deeply into the biblical story to discover the truths about him. John Wesley also used the phrase to name what it means for us to interact with the Word of God as a means of grace.

When Emily and I started reading Bible stories to Alice, I'm not sure we had anything more in mind than a desire for her to become familiar with major characters in the Bible. What we discovered, though, was that she was being formed by those stories right from the beginning. She was being changed by what she heard. The Bible, without us even realizing it, was becoming a means of grace to her.

Searching the Scriptures in the Biblical Witness

Think for a moment what it must have been like to grow up as a Hebrew in ancient times. At some point you would have realized how odd your life was compared to other people. Everybody around you just assumed that there were many gods. Yet your faith taught you that there was only one God—and that this God has a special love for Israel, even though Israel was never large or powerful. Then there was the law to follow. You would have been taught to embrace all kinds of rules regarding diet, ritual cleanliness, and the like that other people would find simply perplexing.

At some point I imagine you would have asked somebody the questions, "Hey, why in the world does our faith require so much of us? And why do we do things that make us so strange in the eyes of the world?"

The answer for these very understandable questions is found in the Bible itself. In chapter 6 of Deuteronomy, Moses explains to the people he's leading through the wilderness that it's going to be important for them to tell their children the story of their faith.

Look, Moses says to the parents, *there's going to come a time when your children approach you with questions. They're going to want to know why we have all these strange laws and rituals.*

Like any parent, Moses knows that it won't be enough to just tell the kids what to do. They're going to want reasons. So he continues. *When they ask you about all these things, you tell them this: we were Pharaoh's slaves in Egypt. And the L*ORD *brought us out of there with a mighty hand. He brought us out of Egypt so that he could bring us into the Promised Land. Everything we do now—every single one of these laws and rituals—is meant to remind us of God's salvation and our identity as God's people. We have a story with God, and every one of his commands reminds us of that!*

Notice the idea that Moses is trying to get across: God's Word is meant to work goodness in your life. Everything that God has given to us in Holy Scripture is intended to be a means of grace to us. That's why he tells the Hebrews to pass on all the words he has given them: "You shall teach them diligently to your children, and shall talk of them when you sit in your house, and when you walk by the way, and when you lie down, and when you rise" (Deut. 6:6–7).

> "He humbled you by letting you hunger, then by feeding you with manna . . . in order to make you understand that one does not live by bread alone, but by every word that comes from the mouth of the LORD."
> —Deuteronomy 8:3 NRSV

Moses is the first great prophet of the Old Testament. He speaks the word of God, to give spiritual nourishment to God's people. This is what all the subsequent prophets do as well—Isaiah and Jeremiah, Amos and Micah—as they are sent by the Lord to guide Israel toward faithfulness.

The prophets are the mouthpieces of God's word to his people.

When we turn to the New Testament, we find Jesus speaking about the power of the Scriptures as well. Once when Jesus was in Jerusalem teaching, he confronted his audience with a stark claim about the Bible's message. "You search the Scriptures because you think that in them you have eternal life," Jesus says to them, "And it is they that bear witness about me." Then he adds, "Yet you refuse to come to me that you may have life" (John 5:39–40).[1]

It's a profound moment in the Gospels. Christ calls his listeners (then and now) to read the whole of the Bible as pointing to himself. All that God is doing, all that Israel and the church have been struggling toward, all that the promise of salvation contains—these are all bound up in the life of Jesus Christ. He isn't trying to take authority away from the Scriptures. Far from it. He's actually giving the Scriptures even more authority by claiming that they are pointing to the very source of life and salvation. Himself.

Jesus' teaching is important if we want to understand how the Word of God is present in the words of the Bible. It isn't the ink and paper that makes the difference. Rather, it is the presence of God's message within the Bible that is important. When the apostle Paul wrote to his assistant Timothy about the Scriptures, he said that they are "breathed out by God" and useful "for teaching, for reproof, for correction, and for training in righteousness" (2 Tim. 3:16). Paul was talking about the *teaching* contained within Scripture, the teaching of God's good news about the Lord Jesus Christ. God has spoken to us in the person of Jesus Christ, and God still speaks through the revelation of his word in the Bible.

This means that to understand the power of Holy Scripture, we must take it seriously in our study and devotion. Immerse ourselves in it. Become familiar with it. Commit ourselves to reading it with purpose. Learning a verse here and there, or half paying attention during the Sunday sermon in a casual, as-you-feel-like-it-sort-of-way is not going to get you very far. What we need is to embrace the Scripture as the very thing that points us to Christ. As Jesus tells us, by searching the Scriptures we can come to him and find true life!

Searching the Scriptures in Wesleyan Spirituality

I find it interesting that John Wesley never says, "The Bible is a means of grace." Instead, he says that the means of grace is "searching the Scriptures." Is there a difference?

Yes there is a difference, actually. The difference has to do with *how* something can be a means of grace for us. Objects are not means of grace. They are just things. If we focus on the things themselves, we are likely to make idols out of them. Take the Bible, for example. You can walk around with it under your arm every day of your life, but it won't do you any good unless you actually open and read it. Stick it under your pillow at night and sleep on it for forty years and all you'll get is a chronically sore neck. For the word of God that is in Scripture to become a means of grace for us, we have to receive it actively. The means of grace are really about how certain objects and practices are taken up in an active manner in the spiritual life. We must engage them with our minds and our hearts.

When Wesley describes the major approaches to searching the Scriptures, he uses the words *reading*, *hearing*, and *meditating*. He explains what he means like this:

> Reading: Constantly, some part of every day? Regularly, all the Bible in order? . . . Seriously, with prayer before and after? Fruitfully, immediately practicing what you learn there?

> Hearing: Every morning? Carefully; with prayer before, at, after? Immediately putting into practice: Have you a New Testament always about you?

> Meditating: At set times? By any rule?[2]

Wesley's point is that a variety of ways exist for how we can embrace the Word of God. And we can read the Bible on our own in study and devotional contexts. In fact, this is probably the best foundation for how to place God's Word at the center of your life. It must be read daily with an approach that allows each day's reading to build off of the one before it.[3]

One of the things we find in Wesley's teaching on how the Scriptures can be a means of grace in our lives is a deep optimism about the power of God's Word to affect us in every stage of our lives. He claims that searching the Scriptures is "a means of conveying the grace of God to all, whether *unbelievers* . . . or *believers*."[4] The Scriptures can be a means of grace to unbelievers because they contain the good news itself. They serve as the vessel for God's Word— the way that the Christian message of faith and forgiveness gets communicated. For those who already believe, scriptural teaching maintains its power to transform human life.

When we receive forgiveness we experience a new birth, but that rebirth is but the first step toward our completion in Christ. So we are called to search the Scriptures throughout our lives, as God continues to renew us in ever-greater ways.

Wesley's great concern in how he understands the Bible to function as a means of grace is always that we would see the connection between Spirit and word. He says that "all outward means whatever, if separate from the Spirit of God, cannot profit at all, cannot conduce in any degree either to the knowledge or love of God."[5] So there is no power in the letter of the text itself, except the power that comes by the Holy Spirit. Yet, the Holy Spirit will also never disagree with anything in the word of Scripture. So the key to searching the Scriptures faithfully is in trusting God's promise to give us the Spirit as our guide and counselor. We can trust in the means of grace because we trust that God will meet us in the means as he has promised to do.[6]

Searching the Scriptures in Our Daily Discipleship

We recently began a new Bible study at my church. I'm leading a group of about twenty people through the Gospel of Luke. We're going to take four months to work through Luke from start to finish, reading the entire book slowly and carefully.

During our first meeting, I asked the people who joined what they hoped to get out of the study.

The answers told me a lot about how believers hunger for the sustenance of God's Word. Here are some of their responses:

- "I want to learn more about God's Word."
- "For a closer, more personal relationship with Jesus Christ."
- "I am interested to know more about the content of the Bible."
- "I like the idea of the benefits of a group Bible study. We can learn more from one another's perspectives on the biblical material. And we can also benefit spiritually from the relationships that will form in our group."
- "To learn the ways of Jesus."

I think these are all wonderful reasons to commit to searching the Scriptures. The common element that I see in all of those responses is this: they all desire to embrace Holy Scripture as a means of grace.

Perhaps the most important point to realize about taking our study of the Bible more seriously is that we don't study the Bible in order to master it. We study the Bible so that it might master us. That means that the first thing we need to do in approaching the Scriptures is to come with the right attitude—a willingness to humble ourselves, open our hearts and minds to Christ Jesus, and ask that the Holy Spirit be present in the midst of our study.

Remember the apostle Paul's description of the nature of the Scriptures: "breathed out by God." The Bible's power is a spiritual power, meaning that it comes from the presence of the Holy Spirit working through it. In order for that power to transform us within, we need to set aside all our presuppositions and claims and agenda items so that a space is made for the Spirit to do what the Spirit will. Prayer is a central part of taking on that attitude. So in other words, the first step in adopting the discipline of searching the Scriptures as a means of grace is *humility*.

When we move from preparation to practice, we should recognize that it is possible to search the Scriptures in a number of different ways. The Wesleyan approach to this calls our attention to the three elements of reading, hearing, and meditating on Scripture. I think of these three elements as connected to three common discipleship activities:

1. Reading . . . connected to . . . personal study
2. Hearing . . . connected to . . . worship (sermons) and group Bible study
3. Meditating . . . connected to . . . spiritual contemplation

When we put personal study, worship and fellowship with others, and spiritual contemplation together, we have the framework for how to embrace the Bible as a means of grace in every part of our spiritual lives.

The first part of searching the Scriptures involves personally opening your Bible and reading it on a regular basis. This is easy to understand, but for many people it can also be intimidating. The word "Bible" means "book," but the Bible is actually a collection of sixty-six books, written down over the course of many centuries and consisting of a lot of different types of literature. It has history, genealogy, and chronicle. It has poetry,

> We don't study the Bible in order to master it. We study the Bible so that it might master us.

prophecy, and proverbs. There are letters and gospels and apocalyptic visions. Many of the place names sound strange, and the names of people can be even stranger. The study Bible on my desk right now runs to more than

2,700 pages! It's no wonder that a common experience of pastors is for their church members to admit to them that they find the Bible hard to understand and more than a little daunting.

When I started to read the Bible seriously for the first time, it was important for me to find ways to make it seem more manageable. Devotional guides can do that, and Bible commentaries do it at a more advanced level. While a devotional guide often focuses on a topical approach to Bible study, I think it is also important for people to get a sense of the flow and scope of whole books of the Bible. The Scriptures weren't written in little two- or three-verse chunks, after all. They were written as whole books. For me, that means reading them as whole books is the best way to get a sense of the message contained within them. Fortunately, there are plenty of study materials available to guide a reader through the Bible in a manageable way.[7] The key to personal Bible study beyond finding a good study resource, of course, is committing to a daily discipline.

The second part of searching the Scriptures has to do with hearing them spoken and described by other people. The most common form of hearing the Scriptures for most Christians is through a sermon or homily during Sunday worship. I think that this form of searching has to be a cornerstone of any Christian's engagement with the Bible. Most preachers work very hard on their sermons in ways that are not always obvious to a congregation. They read the Scripture passage they will be preaching upon over and over again. They pray about it. And they consult biblical commentaries by scholars and pastors who offer their interpretations on it. Then they reflect on how to put the message of that Scripture passage in a relatable context, including illustrations that help to shed light on aspects of the biblical message. So if you really focus on what a preacher is saying in the context of a sermon, you are likely to receive spiritual food that can sustain you throughout the week.

Another way we can search the Scriptures by hearing them is through participating in a group Bible study. When we do that, we have the advantage of listening to the reflections and interpretations of other people who have read and prayed about the same Scriptures we have been studying. My own primary work at present is a teaching ministry, which I do both in seminary and church contexts. I love teaching the Bible in a group study format at my church because of the tremendous gift I receive from all the people in the Bible study. Personal Bible reading is very important, but so is searching the Scriptures in fellowship with other Christians. (In fact, I believe we are much more likely to stick to our personal discipline of daily reading when we are also involved in a group Bible study.)

The third way we can search the Scriptures is through meditating upon them. This may be the least obvious approach to many people, but it can also be among the most fruitful. How you go about meditating upon Scripture can be understood in different ways. For many people, it will be through pondering a preacher's message during the Sunday sermon. Others like to focus on memory verses, which they will commit to mind and then repeat in a reflective manner. I do this sometimes when I am mowing the lawn or running on the treadmill. One of my favorite passages for meditation is Proverbs 3:5–6, "Trust in the LORD with all your heart, and rely not on your own insight. In all your ways acknowledge him, and he will make straight your paths" (NRSV). I have also known people who find benefit in reading the Scripture in a meditative manner. They will select a Scripture passage and then read it slowly, again and again, often stopping to offer a prayer for God to illumine the mind and heart to understand the Scripture's meaning more fully. By reading in a contemplative way, we are reminded that engaging the Bible is not just about learning its content. It is instead about sitting with God's Word, allowing time for the Spirit to meet us there. In our present culture and its unlimited distractions, shutting off all our devices and opening up the Bible can be one of the most important things we can do.

CHAPTER 4

Prayer

THE URGE TO REACH OUT TO OTHERS IS ONE OF our strongest instincts. It's as basic as our need for food or sleep. We need to communicate with other people. We need to connect with others and to be understood. We reach out to other people to love and be loved because all of us have an innate desire for relationship.

When we begin to talk about prayer, we are really just talking about finding this same kind of personal connection with God. A noted Bible resource points out that all Christian prayer is "conditioned by the biblical understanding of God as a personal being who hears the prayers of his people."[1] In other words, the God we worship is not an impersonal deity! He is not a distant creator far removed from the lives of his creatures. God is instead a loving God, whose "will is ever directed to his children's good."[2] This God is the God revealed to us in the Scriptures as Father, Son, and Holy Spirit. And this God wants us to know him, as he knows us.

I have found that prayer can seem like an intimidating thing to some people. I've been told more than once by people struggling with personal or spiritual issues that they don't know how to pray, or else that they've tried praying but were afraid they "weren't doing it right." So let me offer a simple definition for prayer right here at the outset: prayer is the act of lifting up our thoughts, words, and affections to God. It is a kind of conversation with God, where we both speak and listen.

If prayer is a conversation with God, then obviously it has to involve our own thoughts and words. But I've also said that it involves our affections—and I use that word intentionally rather than a word like "emotions." An emotion is something that we just experience; it emerges out of us unbidden. But an affection is a bit different. Affections of the heart traditionally have been things that can be shaped or molded. Good or holy affections like love and generosity are those we would want to nurture in our lives. Other affections are not so good: timidity, meanness of spirit, or greed. All affections are appropriate to offer up before God, though, because it is God who can give a greater shape to our good affections and can diminish our negative affections. Plus, our affections are also just part of us—as much as our thoughts and words are. They are part of how we communicate with others. So they ought to be a part of how we communicate with God too.

Christians believe that prayer can satisfy a deep yearning of our hearts. Saint Augustine spoke to this yearning at the beginning of his autobiography, *The Confessions*. He prayed to God, "You have made us for yourself, and our hearts are restless until they rest in you." Each

> Prayer is the act of lifting up our thoughts, words, and affections to God.

of us has had the breath of God breathed into us. God has created us in his own image. And we're never really home until we're home with God.

Prayer in the Biblical Witness

Prayer shows up all throughout the Bible. If prayer is heartfelt conversation with God, then we find it as early as Adam's interactions with God in the garden of Eden. We also see it as late as the prayer for Jesus Christ to return again in glory at the end of the book of Revelation. There are countless examples of individuals offering up prayers to God within the Bible. And there is a whole book of the Bible—the Psalms—that is made up entirely of prayers.

One of the consistent themes in the New Testament's teaching about prayer is that we can be assured that God will hear and respond to our prayers. The apostle John points to this when he says, "This is the confidence we have in approaching God: that if we ask anything according to his will, he hears us" (1 John 5:14 NIV). This is a wonderful message! It tells us that God knows our needs, and that God absolutely expects us to bring our needs to him through prayer.

One way to think about prayer in the Bible is to look at the different types of prayers that we find. Perhaps the easiest way to think about the major biblical modes of prayer is through the acronym "ACTS." It stands for Adoration, Confession, Thanksgiving, and Supplication. The four types of prayer that go by these names are found in many places in the Bible.

A *prayer of adoration* is a prayer that praises God's goodness and majesty. In the Bible, we find prayers of adoration in the Psalms, which are often called psalms of praise. For instance, Psalm 111:

> Praise the LORD!
> I will give thanks to the LORD with my whole heart,
>   in the company of the upright, in the
>   congregation.
> Great are the works of the LORD,
>   studied by all who delight in them.
> Full of honor and majesty is his work,
>   and his righteousness endures forever.
> He has gained renown by his wonderful deeds;
>   the LORD is gracious and merciful.
>
> (vv. 1–4 NRSV)

A *prayer of confession* is a searching prayer of the heart. When we confess, we bare our souls before God about our sins and shortcomings. Confession to God is also a model for the kind of mutual confession that believers in the body of Christ are called upon to make to one another (see James 5:16). But ultimately, since all sin is sin against God, we are called to confess our sins to God. A key part of the good news of Jesus is that repentance can bring forgiveness and new life. Indeed, the Bible assures us that sincere confession before God will be met with forgiveness. We see this in 1 John 1:9 which says, "If we confess our sins, he who is faithful and just will forgive us our sins and cleanse us from all unrighteousness" (NRSV). So prayers of confession ought to be a regular part of our spiritual lives, as we become transformed into the people God would have us be.

A *prayer of thanksgiving* is a prayer that recognizes the good things God gives us and offers thanks for them: our lives, our health, our families, and our faith. The apostle

Paul told us, "Rejoice always, pray without ceasing, give thanks in all circumstances; for this is the will of God in Christ Jesus for you" (1 Thess. 5:16–18 NRSV). A part of what it means to live faithfully is to live out of a deep sense of gratitude for all that God has done for us. Prayers of thanksgiving help us to do that. They give proper thanks to God and also shape us into thankful people at our core.

A *prayer of supplication* is a prayer that lifts up requests before God. Supplications are often divided between those requests we make for ourselves (petitions) and those requests we make on behalf of other people (intercessions). We can turn again to the apostle Paul, who told us in Philippians, "Do not worry about anything, but with prayer and supplication with thanksgiving let your requests be made known to God" (v. 4:6 NRSV). It is natural for us to ask God for the desires of our hearts, and we can be assured that God will answer our prayers. Just so, we feel the need to pray on behalf of others as well—our family and friends, as well as those whose needs we know even if we do not know them personally. God does answer prayer, even if we need to be mindful that God's answers to prayer are not always the answers we want God to give!

There are other types of prayer in Scripture beyond the four in the ACTS model. Anyone familiar with the Psalms will know that prayers of lament make up a great part of the Psalter. These lament prayers are a particular type of prayer all their own. In addition, there are particular kinds of prayers of invocation in the Bible, calling upon God to be present in special ways. Prayers of healing fit into this category, as when the letter of James refers to the "prayer of faith" that can heal the sick (see James 5:13–15). Even so, becoming familiar with the ACTS prayers is a great way to become more familiar with biblical models of prayer in general.

When we consider prayer as one of the means of grace, our focus turns to the way Jesus shows us how to pray through his teaching and example in the Gospels. We shouldn't be surprised to learn that Jesus' ministry is filled with prayer. He prays in the wilderness after his baptism. He heals a man through prayer. He teaches his disciples to pray. He withdraws to lonely places when he gets over- whelmed by the crowds so he can reconnect to the Father through prayer. He prays at Gethsemane so he might have strength to face his coming crucifixion. And he even dies with the prayer on his lips, "Into your hands I commend my spirit."

Jesus' life and ministry are clothed in prayer. In that, he offers us a model of how to live as his followers. He invites us to be a people of prayer.

We also find when we go to the Gospels that Jesus wants us to pray as well. The most precious prayer that we can pray is the prayer that Jesus taught to his disciples. It is called the Lord's Prayer or the "Our Father." It looks like this:

> Our Father, who art in heaven,
>   hallowed be thy name,
> Thy kingdom come,
>   thy will be done,
>   on earth as it is in heaven.
> Give us this day our daily bread.
> Forgive us our trespasses
>   as we forgive those who trespass against us.
> And lead us not into temptation,
>   but deliver us from evil

For thine is the kingdom, and the power, and the
   glory,
   for ever and ever. Amen.

We find Jesus teaching this prayer to his disciples in both Matthew 6:7–15 and Luke 11:1–4. If we want to be counted amongst his disciples today, we ought to offer this prayer to God daily.

Prayer in Wesleyan Spirituality

John Wesley believed that the means of grace are given to us because they are the "means of drawing near to God."[3] Wesley's belief about the power of the means of grace echoes Scripture: "Draw near to God, and he will draw near to you" (James 4:8).

We can see how important prayer is when we think about it as a kind of conversation with God. Think about it: if you want to really get to know another person, you have to build a relationship with that person. And the way you do that is by relating to that other person through language! In this day and age, we can communicate in dozens of different ways: from letter writing to phone calling to text messaging, and from e-mailing to photo sharing via social media. There are new apps being developed every day to facilitate communication between people. But none of these ways can ultimately take the place of face-to-face, personal conversation. A teacher of mine once observed, "If you want to get to really know another person, you have to listen to his story. And then you have to share your story in return." We learn God's story with us as it is revealed in Scripture. And we share our story with God through prayer. In this way, we draw near to God and God draws near to us.

One of the ways we can learn about the Wesleyan way of prayer is through the teaching that Wesley himself made about prayer. They include the way that prayer gives us these three gifts: encouragement, assurance, and transformation.

Wesley's teaching about *encouragement* in prayer is based on the notion that God's desire for relationship with us always comes by way of invitation rather than coercion. That is, the very nature of grace is such that it beckons and invites but does not twist our arms. That is the way love works at all times, and it is especially so with God. Wesley's teaching on prayer is first and foremost to encourage us to be a people of prayer. He says, "God does nothing but in answer to prayer; and even they who have been converted to God, without praying for it themselves (which is exceeding rare), were not without the prayers of others. Every new victory which a soul gains is the effect of a new prayer."[4] When we pray, we are responding to God's gracious offer of a relationship with us.

For Wesley, the view of prayer as our response to God also explains why the apostle Paul encourages us to "pray without ceasing" in 1 Thessalonians 5:16–18. About this, Wesley says, "God's command to 'pray without ceasing' is founded on the necessity we have of His grace to preserve the life of God in the soul, which can no more subsist one moment without it, than the body can without air."[5] If we need God for life and salvation, then we need to enter into a relationship with God that is sustained in every moment of every day. The means to that daily relationship is, above all, through prayer.

The encouragement to pray leads next to an *assurance* that God hears our prayers and answers them. We have already seen John's teaching on that: "This is the confidence we have in approaching God: that if we ask anything according to his will he hears us" (1 John 5:14). Peter echoed him: "Cast all your anxiety on him, because he cares for you" (1 Peter 5:7 NRSV). Wesley's view of assurance through prayer builds off of these biblical foundations. He told us, "On every occasion of uneasiness we should retire to prayer, that we may give place to the grace and light of God, and then form our resolutions, without being in any pain about what success they may have. . . . In the greatest temptations, a single look to Christ, and the barely pronouncing His name, suffices to overcome the wicked one, so it be done with confidence and calmness of spirit."[6] This does not mean we will always get the answers we want, of course. But it does mean that God hears our prayers and responds. It means we can be assured of the most important need that we have: namely, that God will be present with us and will save us.

Finally, the Wesleyan view of prayer contains within it a belief in God's *transformation* through prayer. By nurturing our relationship with God, Wesley says, we "unite ourselves to God, in whom the soul expands itself in prayer."[7] He expresses this view beautifully in his sermon, "The New Birth," when he writes about what the believer's life looks like once he is born again by God's grace:

> God is continually breathing, as it were, upon his soul, and his soul is breathing unto God. Grace is descending into his heart, and prayer and praise ascending to heaven. And by this intercourse between God and man, this fellowship with the Father and the Son, as by a kind of spiritual

respiration, the life of God in the soul is sustained: and the child of God grows up, till he comes to "the full measure of the stature of Christ."[8]

What Wesley calls an "intercourse between God and man" amounts to a rich description of the life of prayer. God pours out his grace into our hearts, which makes us into new people. We then offer what we have to God—which is our prayer and praise in thanksgiving for what God has done for us. This isn't something that happens only once, of course. Wesley describes is as "spiritual respiration." It is like breathing, something that simply comes to mark us as new creatures. And the effect in us is a deep transformation, where we come to love God and neighbor with all that we are.

Prayer in Our Daily Discipleship

When I was seven years old, my parents bought me my first bicycle. It was glorious—a yellow and red bike with a banana seat and tassels coming off of the handlebars. The best part about it was the big Spiderman shield attached right on the front of the handlebars. It was a Spidey bike! And I loved it the minute I set eyes on it.

The problem with a present like your first bicycle is that to really enjoy it, you have to learn how to ride it. And that took awhile. I used to get my dad to go outside into the driveway with me after he got home from work. I would get on and start peddling, and he'd hold the metal ring at the back of that banana seat, walking along behind me and keeping me upright.

It took awhile before he could let go of the back of my bike without me toppling over. And it took even longer before I could hop up on the bike and start peddling down the driveway without a second thought about my balance. But eventually that's what happens with riding a bicycle: you get to the point that you can ride it without thinking about what you are actually doing. Balance, peddling, and steering all just get integrated into your experience to the point where it becomes second nature.

Prayer is not terribly different from learning to ride a bicycle. It can seem difficult at first, even unnatural. It can certainly help to have someone more experienced offer a guiding hand. Of course, it requires practice. But over time, it becomes more and more familiar until doing it becomes second nature to daily life. It will help us now to look at what "second-nature" prayer looks like, as well as some of the ways we can think about adopting prayer into our daily discipleship.

One of my favorite descriptions of prayer comes from the early church father Clement of Alexandria, who said, "Prayer, to speak somewhat boldly, is converse with God. Even if we address Him in a whisper, without opening our lips, or uttering a sound, still we cry to Him in our heart. For God never ceases to listen to the inward converse of the heart."[9] I think this description fits with my own experience with prayer, which is that sometimes I don't feel like I have the right words to speak to God to describe the deep longings of my heart. In fact, it is often at the times I feel the need to be closest to God that I have the trouble finding the language to pray.

In Romans, Paul said, "We do not know what to pray for as we ought, but the Spirit himself intercedes for us with groanings too deep for words" (Rom. 8:26). In this way, God searches our hearts and hears our longings even when we don't know how to speak them aloud. I find great assurance in this point of view, because it tells me that God is often closest to me when I am in the midst of my greatest struggles.

Clearly, we need to practice how we pray. If we want to become a people of prayer, then we need to engage in prayer both daily and in a variety of ways. Wesley believed in both written prayers and prayers of the heart. He thought it was essential for Christians to pray together in worship, but he also believed strongly in the value of personal prayer time. He also valued what he called "family prayer." He counseled people to pray "every morning and evening," by which he meant upon rising in the morning and before going to sleep at night.[11] He encouraged them to pray to God in such a way that they "lift up thy heart to him, to pour out thy soul before him."[12] In other words, he believed that the true Christian life was a life of prayer.

> "Prayer is the lifting up of the heart to God: all words of prayer without this are mere hypocrisy. Whenever therefore thou attemptest to pray, see that it be thy one design to commune with God, to lift up thy heart to him, to pour out thy soul before him."
>
> —John Wesley[10]

The Wesleyan approach to prayer should lead us to think about a number of possibilities for the practice of prayer in our own discipleship. Let me offer three:

1. We should approach the kind of prayer we do in worship services seriously. When we pray the Lord's Prayer, we should remember that this is the prayer Jesus has

taught us to pray. When we confess our sins before God with the rest of our congregation, we should focus on the words we say, recognizing that there is great value in lifting up our confessions together as the body of Christ. And when our pastors offer prayers for us, we should pay attention to what is actually being prayed, remembering that this is a collective prayer that we are all offering up together.

2. We should make private prayer a daily habit. Wesley's advice about praying upon waking in the morning and praying before going to bed at night is helpful. Such times of the day are excellent points to remember with thankfulness all that God has given us. Praying in the morning prepares us for the day and helps us to adopt "the same mind that was in Christ Jesus" (Phil. 2:5 NRSV). Praying at night is a way to recollect the day we have just spent, examining ourselves and offering up our adoration, confession, thanksgiving, and supplication to God.

3. We should make a concerted attempt to engage in family prayer, both at mealtimes and at a set-aside time with our spouses and children. In my experience, this is one of the most neglected opportunities for prayer that is before us. It is too easy to allow a mealtime blessing to become a perfunctory prayer, when in fact it is a time for the family to offer its earnest thanksgivings to God. Children also should be taught the practice and discipline of prayer, and their parents are by far the best people to do that. A time for family prayer in the evening should be a staple of any family's devotion. It is something that can become a building block for faith in the young.

One of the types of prayer that I was introduced to some years ago is called a "breath prayer." It is a kind of prayer that I pray often now, and it has helped me to pray much more regularly in general. In a breath prayer, a simple prayer of only one or two sentences can be said over and over until it becomes a rhythm. One breath prayer that I pray when I am in the shower, driving to work, exercising, or mowing the yard, goes like this: "Lord Jesus Christ, Son of God, have mercy on me, a sinner."[13] I've found that this prayer draws me to Christ and helps me to internalize the practice of prayer in a wonderful way.

Wesley once said, "In souls filled with love, the desire to please God is a continual prayer."[14] This should be our aim in practicing prayer as a means of grace—that our entire being would become a prayer offered up to God. By embracing prayer in this way, we can come to know the kind of spiritual life that Wesley talks about. We can come to know the presence of the Holy Spirit as close as our own breath.

CHAPTER 5

The Lord's Supper

A FEW YEARS AGO I WAS APPOINTED TO PASTOR A small church while I was in graduate school. The congregation had been served by a lay speaker for several years prior to my arrival. He was a true saint of a man—every bit the minister I was and more. But since he was not ordained, he didn't administer the Lord's Supper during worship. When I arrived I spoke to the congregation about moving to a monthly practice of Holy Communion, and everyone was eager to do that.

On the first Communion Sunday, I led the church through the liturgy. In my tradition, that always includes Jesus' words of institution: "This is my body, this is my blood. Do this in remembrance of me." As I spoke these words before the congregation, I held up the bread and the cup of wine so the congregation could see them. Once our prayers were finished and the invitation to come forward was given, the people began to leave their pews and file forward. My wife, Emily, ended up behind a family with a nine-year-old girl. This family was at church every Sunday, but most of the girl's life she had not been able to experience the Lord's Supper. As the line moved forward, my wife saw the girl tug on her mother's sleeve and look up at her. "Is it *really* blood, Mama?" she asked with wide eyes.

I smile every time I think back on that story. The sense of awe and mystery that my little nine-year-old church member felt approaching the altar was exactly right. The sacrament itself goes by a number of names: Holy Communion, Eucharist, the Lord's Supper. All of them refer to the most central act of worship in which Christians partake. John Wesley taught that Jesus Christ gave the Lord's Supper to the early church as "the grand channel whereby the grace of his Spirit was conveyed to the souls of all the children of God."[1]

Along with baptism, we call the Lord's Supper by a special term: *sacrament*. It's a word that refers to something that is holy. And indeed, the Lord's Supper is a holy meal. It is a meal that constitutes the church, in a certain sense. It provides us with the most vivid image of what God calls the church to be: the fellowship of Jesus' disciples gathered together around a table in his name, celebrating his sacrifice, and receiving the sustenance of his grace. As much as anything we can do, the Lord's Supper is a true means of grace.

The Lord's Supper in the Biblical Witness

If we want to understand the power and meaning of the Lord's Supper, we have to start by going back to the Old Testament. Before the twelve tribes of Israel settled the land of Canaan, their ancestors lived as slaves in Egypt. Pharaoh was a cruel master, and he eventually conspired to kill all Hebrew boys at birth. Then God called a man named Moses to be his prophet and liberate the Hebrews from slavery. Through Moses, God showed his power to Pharaoh by bringing about ten terrible plagues upon Egypt. The worst of these was the last—the Lord would sweep over the land and kill all the firstborn in Egypt.

The Hebrew people were told how to avoid this plague. They were to sacrifice a lamb and spread its blood on their doorposts. Then God would see that sign and pass over the homes of the Hebrews, sparing their own firstborn. It was this terrible judgment by God that finally convinced Pharaoh to allow the Hebrews' escape from Egypt. Since that time, the people of Israel have remembered and celebrated God's deliverance through the Passover meal.

It was this same Passover meal that caused Jesus to call together his disciples on the night of his betrayal. He wanted to celebrate the Passover with them, but he wanted to add something more to it. Following the meal on that night in the upper room, Jesus took a loaf of bread and cup of wine and prepared to give a gift to the church.

Now, let's pause just a moment. I think we have to remember how significant Jesus' actions were on that night. He knew his time was at hand. He knew he had one last shot with the disciples. He could have done anything with them—taught them anything he wanted, given them particular instructions. What he chose to do was to gather them together for the Passover meal in the upper room. And he chose to give his closest companions a gift that was meant for the church in all the generations to follow.

As the Bible tells it, after the Passover meal had been eaten Jesus took a loaf of bread. Then he broke the bread and gave it to his disciples, saying, "Take and eat, this is my body which is given for you. Do this in remembrance of me." After they had received the bread, Jesus took a cup of wine. "This cup that is poured out for you is the new covenant in my blood," he said (see Luke 22:19–20). And then he shared the cup of wine with them as well. All of this happened just hours before Jesus was betrayed by Judas Iscariot and handed over to be interrogated, beaten, condemned, and finally crucified.

The lamb that Hebrew families sacrificed on the night of the tenth plague foreshadows the sacrifice of Jesus Christ. He is the one that Revelation identifies as the Lamb that has been slaughtered and yet now sits upon the throne of heaven. This Lamb, Revelation tells us, will be our shepherd. He will guide us to the springs of the water of life, and he will wipe every tear from our eyes (v. 7:17). At the Last Supper, the disciples—all of them Jews—would have been reminded of the sacrificial lambs in Egypt when they ate the Passover meal with Jesus that night. Through his teaching to them, he prepared them to remember his own sacrifice on the cross that was still to come. Even so, Jesus wants us to think about the sacrifice of himself when we celebrate the Lord's Supper now.

"For indeed Christ, our Passover, was sacrificed for us. Therefore let us keep the feast, not with old leaven, nor with the leaven of malice and wickedness, but with the unleavened bread of sincerity and truth."

—1 Corinthians 5:7b–8 NKJV

When we see John Wesley calling the Lord's Supper the grand channel of God's grace to us, he is emphasizing the deep importance it has in uniting the Christian faith with the faith of Israel. Jesus chose a very particular moment to share the gift of Holy Communion—both to show its connection to the Passover meal and to show the disciples how central it ought to be to the practice of the Christian faith. Through the Lord's Supper, Jesus tells us that his story is the culmination of Israel's story. And he gives us a place in that story by sharing the holy meal with us and commanding us to share it with others forever after. It is the symbol of his saving death, the most powerful expression of God's love for us.

The Lord's Supper in Wesleyan Spirituality

Earlier we saw how Wesley does not say that the Bible itself is a means of grace. Instead, he says "searching the Scriptures" is the means of grace. He focuses on the activity of searching rather than the object itself because it is in the process of engaging God's word with our minds and hearts that we encounter the Holy Spirit.

With that in mind, it shouldn't be a surprise that Wesley does not typically say, "The Lord's Supper is a means of grace." If he were to do that, it might lead us to focus too much on the physical objects: bread and wine. So Wesley favors action verbs in his teaching on the Lord's Supper. He talks about "partaking of the Lord's Supper" and "receiving the Lord's Supper."[2] He wants us to think about encountering the power of the Holy Spirit in the midst of worship, in other words. Without God's presence through the power of the Spirit, the bread and wine remain just bread and wine. But with the Spirit, they become the body and blood of Christ for us.

There's a little bit of a disconnect between the way that Wesley viewed Holy Communion and the way it has been viewed by many Wesleyans and Methodists in subsequent generations. After the Methodist movement crossed the Atlantic Ocean and ended up as a separate church following the American Revolution, the sacramental focus of Wesley's teaching was largely lost. Eventually, most Methodist churches were celebrating the Lord's Supper quarterly (four times per year). There were reasons for this development—the spread-out, frontier character of early America (with too few ordained ministers) not least among them. Nevertheless, it was still a far cry from Wesley's counsel that "every Christian should receive the Lord's Supper as often as he can."[3] He taught that we should celebrate Holy Communion at every opportunity.

Why so often? Wesley believed that the rationale for celebrating Holy Communion as often as possible comes from two points of biblical teaching. The first point is the *command* from Jesus when he says, "Do this in remembrance of me." The idea here is that his command is ongoing. We don't just "do this" one time and consider that to be the end of the matter. Instead, Jesus expects us to "do this" over and over again, and this is supported in Scripture by the frequency that the Lord's Supper is celebrated in the Acts of the Apostles. It is also supported by the way the apostle Paul teaches about the Lord's Supper in his writings. So if we want to be faithful to the command of Christ Jesus, we will receive the Lord's Supper as often as possible.

The second point that helps us understand why we should celebrate often comes from the effects upon us of receiving the Lord's Supper. It's here that the real power of Communion as a means of grace can be seen. It makes Jesus Christ's forgiveness of our sins real to us—for it is out of forgiving love, after all, that he says, "This is my body, given for you." The Lord's Supper is also intended, Wesley says, for the "strengthening and refreshing of our souls." His description of the sacrament's power on this point is remarkable. Bread and wine are food that we can eat to nourish our bodies. But *this* bread and wine—the bread and wine of the sacrament—is meant to be "the food of our souls." They give us the "strength to believe, to love and obey God." His language is vivid, and it is all meant to convey an understanding of how Holy Communion really is a means of grace to us.[4]

There are a number of ways that we can understand how the Lord's Supper acts as a means of grace. These ways are reflected in the words of the liturgy for Holy Communion: "Christ has died, Christ is risen, Christ will come again." The first of these has to do with the way that Communion *gives us the memory* of all that Jesus Christ was and did. That's the most direct meaning of Jesus' words to "Do this in remembrance of me." We remember that God became incarnate in the person of Jesus. We remember his teaching, his preaching, and his healing. We especially remember his sacrifice upon the cross for our sins. As we eat and drink from the bread and the cup, we remember that his body and blood were given *for us*.

Yet even though we know that Christ has died, we also know that Christ is risen. He was raised from the dead, and he will be alive forevermore. So the second way that the Lord's Supper is a means of grace to us is in the way that it *conveys the power of his grace to us now*. When Wesley describes the Lord's Supper as the food for our souls, he is saying that it offers us something real in the here and now. In my own experience I can testify that the Lord's Supper does indeed convey a spiritual power unlike any other.

When I attended my first summer youth program as a junior high–schooler, I was mostly excited about spending a few nights away from home and having fun. We had plenty of fun that summer, but I also encountered the power of the Holy Spirit in a way I never had before in my life. At the end of an evening worship service, we received Holy Communion and gathered on an outdoor patio to sing quiet songs of praise to Jesus Christ. I had been partaking of the Lord's Supper for as long as I could remember, but something was different about that night. Something entered my heart and soul unlike anything I had ever known as I went forward to receive the bread and the cup. During our time in quiet song afterward, this power overwhelmed me and I felt as if I were melting from the inside out. Tears flowed down my cheeks. The inward experience was one of indescribable joy. I had heard Jesus Christ preached and taught for my entire life in church. At that moment, though, I *knew* that Jesus Christ was real through his grace given to me. It's an experience that has remained with me every day since, and the means by which it was given was the sacrament of Holy Communion.

The final confession in the liturgy is that Christ will come again. This points us to the third way that the Lord's Supper acts as a means of grace for us. This is because the Lord's Supper stands as *a sign of God's promise*. And that promise is that Christ will return in ultimate victory at the end of days. When Wesley wants to emphasize this aspect of the sacrament, he cites the apostle Paul's teaching, "For as often as you eat this bread and drink the cup, you proclaim the Lord's death until he comes" (1 Cor. 11:26). Thus, we can understand Holy Communion "refreshing our souls . . . with the hope of glory."[5] It is a continual reminder of God's promise that Christ is coming back to us to bring all things to completion. In other words, the practice of the Lord's Supper is nothing less than a foretaste of the kingdom to come.[6]

The Lord's Supper in Our Daily Discipleship

When we were looking at prayer and searching the Scriptures, we were looking at examples of the means of grace that can be practiced *either* alone *or* in the context of a community. The Lord's Supper is different in that respect. Celebrating the Lord's Supper is the essence of the whole church's worship. We all receive the bread and the cup individually, but none of us receives it alone. Just as Christ Jesus called the twelve disciples together at the Last Supper so, too, does he call his church together around the altar for Holy Communion now.

When you think about what is happening at Holy Communion, it's like the sacrament is drawing us back in time so that we are, in a sense, joining the twelve disciples around that table in the upper room with Jesus. He is sharing his table with us, and he is including us in the company of his friends. He is offering us himself and in doing that he is making us a part of himself. As Jesus does that, he also shows us that we can share him with those others who are around the table with us. Stanley Hauerwas reminded us, "In this meal we are made part of God's life and thus share our lives with one another."[7]

This element of what Holy Communion means tells us something crucially important about the church itself. The church is, in a sense, the community of those who gather with Jesus around his table to share in the meal he gives us. We want to belong at that table, and of course Jesus tells us that we do. But everyone else gathered there belongs as well—they, too, are the ones to whom Jesus says, "No longer do I call you servants . . . but I have called you friends" (John 15:15). All who partake of his body are now a *part* of his body, and that body is made up of those whom Jesus has given the command, "Love one another: just as I have loved you" (John 13:34). That is the test of true discipleship, Jesus says. We will be known as his disciples when we learn to love one another the same way he has loved us. The implications of this teaching are far-reaching indeed. What the Eucharist invites us to experience is a new form of life where the old ways of the world are replaced by a new community of holy love.

> Celebrating the Lord's Supper is the essence of the church's worship. We all receive the bread and the cup individually, but none of us receives it alone. It is the shared meal of Jesus' friends.

As a seminary professor, I often encouraged my students to focus the entire worship service on the sacrament of Holy Communion whenever it is to be celebrated. That means choosing Communion hymns or praise songs to sing. It means offering up prayers that center on Eucharistic themes. And it means preaching a Holy Communion sermon if that is at all possible. It can be tragic when a congregation starts to see the Lord's Supper as nothing more than a ritual, practiced once a month, that lengthens the worship service by an extra (and unwanted) ten minutes. When that happens, I think it is usually because the congregation has been allowed to think of Holy Communion as nothing more than a duty. Its power has been quenched, usually for lack of good teaching within the worship setting itself.

If we think about the Lord's Supper as the central act of worship Jesus has given us, then it reframes our practice of it entirely. Here I like to think back about that passage in the Acts of the Apostles that was so important to John Wesley's understanding of the means of grace. Through their practices of worship and devotion—including the "breaking of bread"—the early Christians experienced a whole new kind of life. The Bible even says that "awe came upon every soul" and that through these means "the Lord added to their number day by day those who were being saved" (see Acts 2:42–47). That doesn't give you a mathematical formula for how grace works, but it does offer a testimony of its power. Follow the commands of Jesus Christ, and we can be assured that grace will follow us. For Wesley, it is impossible to think that we could partake of the holy meal that Jesus gives us without grace being at the center of it. He puts it this way:

> Is not the eating of that bread, and the drinking of that cup, the outward, visible means whereby God conveys into our souls all that spiritual grace, that righteousness, and peace, and joy in the Holy Ghost, which were purchased by the body of Christ once broken and the blood of Christ once shed for us? Let all, therefore, who truly desire the grace of God, eat of that bread and drink of that cup.[8]

So do we want to experience something new? Do we want to embrace fully the life that Jesus offers us? If so, we must embrace his gift of Holy Communion. Charles Wesley, the great hymn writer and John's younger brother, once wrote, "O the depth of love divine, the unfathomable grace! Who shall say how bread and wine God into us conveys! How the bread his flesh imparts, how the wine transmits his blood, fills his faithful people's hearts with all the life of God!"[9] I like to think of those words as a reminder of the power contained in the gift God is trying to give us. In the Lord's Supper, that is the gift of himself.

CHAPTER 6

Fasting

SOMETIME AFTER THEIR RETURN FROM THE Babylonian exile, there arose among the Jewish people a prophet named Joel. The collection of his prophecies makes up one of the smaller books of the Old Testament. It is remarkable, though, for a particular theme that Joel focused upon: "the day of the LORD." The way that Joel talked about the day of the Lord made it clear that this cataclysmic event would involve God's judgment upon all the peoples of the world. And that judgment may indeed be harsh. "Let all the inhabitants of the land tremble, for the day of the LORD is coming," Joel preached. "It is near, a day of darkness and gloom, a day of clouds and thick darkness!" (Joel 2:1–2). Clearly this isn't the kind of message that would bring a smile to your face if you happened to hear it firsthand.

Though he offered strong words of judgment through his preaching, Joel also said that punishment when the day of the Lord arrives is not inevitable. "'Yet even now,' declares the LORD, 'return to me with all your heart, with fasting, with weeping, and with mourning; and rend your hearts and not your garments'" (Joel 2:12–13). Because God is slow to anger and abounds in steadfast love, he will offer forgiveness if he finds true sorrow and repentance among his people.

Along with the weeping and mourning that Joel mentioned when he was talking about repentance, notice the activity he mentioned right alongside them. It's fasting. Fasting, that most unfashionable of spiritual practices, is given as a core element of true repentance before God. As we'll soon see, different types of fasting go far back into the biblical witness. Fasting, as it turns out, is also considered to be among the instituted means of grace in Wesleyan spirituality. So unfashionable or not, it deserves our serious consideration.

Fasting in the Biblical Witness

The practice of fasting is found throughout the Old Testament, but it isn't done for just one reason. One of the major purposes of fasting was as a form of repentance for unfaithfulness. Fasting could be adopted by individuals whom God condemned for their sin and injustice by one of the prophets. Following his double betrayal of his loyal soldier Uriah, King David was confronted by the prophet Nathan who pronounced judgment over his sin. In response, David undertook a fast of repentance in the hopes that his son by Bathsheba would be spared by God (see 2 Samuel 12:13–16). Later, King Ahab also fasts and puts on sackcloth to show his repentance following Elijah's words of judgment against him for the death of Naboth and the seizure of his vineyard (see 1 Kings 21:27). Of course, fasting could be undertaken by the whole Israelite people as a form of national repentance as well. The Jews fasted, put on sackcloth, and covered their heads with dirt as a sign of their confession and a part of the renewal of the covenant following their return from exile (see Nehemiah 9:1–2). It's also the reason that Joel mentions fasting as a way to show sorrow prior to the coming day of the Lord.

Fasting was undertaken on other occasions as well—not necessarily disconnected from the confession of sin, but for other reasons in addition. Leaders would sometimes proclaim a fast at the approach of war or other danger as a way to seek God's assistance.[1] People also fasted to seek divine assistance for other specific favors, as when Nehemiah combines fasting and prayer when he wants to ask God to restore Israel near the end of exile (see Nehemiah 1:4–11). Sometimes, fasting would be done primarily to show grief in tragic circumstances. David's fast following the deaths of King Saul and his son Jonathan is an example (see 2 Samuel 1:11–12), as is the Jews' fast throughout the Persian Empire when they learn that the royal servant Mordecai has conspired to assassinate them (see Esther 4:1–3).

A final type of fasting in the Old Testament can be seen in the Nazirite vow. The "vow of a Nazirite" is first mentioned in the book of Numbers, where it is described as a temporary consecration that a man or woman can make as a form of purification and special dedication.[2] Nazirites abstain from wine or any other alcoholic beverage during the time of their vow, and they also avoid certain behaviors such as cutting their hair, shaving, or touching a corpse. While not a fast in the traditional sense, the Nazirite vow embraced the spirit of fasting by its self-denial. It was also seen as serious business. The original teaching about the vow was given directly from God to Moses, and when the prophet Amos pronounced God's judgment on Israel sometime in the eighth century BC, one of the people's transgressions was that they "made the Nazirites drink wine" (Amos 2:11–12). A number of figures throughout the Bible take some form of a Nazirite vow. The hero Samson is one (which puts the consequences of his haircut in a whole new light!). The prophet Samuel is another.[3] In the New Testament, the apostle Paul appears to have taken some version of a Nazirite vow during his second missionary journey.[4]

Fasting appears directly in the life and ministry of Jesus Christ in the Gospels. Following Jesus' baptism in the River Jordan, he went out into the wilderness for forty days. It was a period of fasting and temptation for Jesus, who was "full of the Holy Spirit" and "ate nothing during those days" (Luke 4:1–2). When Satan came to test him, he specifically aimed at Jesus' practice of fasting. He knew Jesus would be weak from hunger and tempted him to turn a stone into bread. Jesus' response was to quote the Torah, saying, "Man does not live by bread alone." He fasted from food so that he might be nourished by God the Father; he was the very Word of God and so knew the truth that God's children are called to live "by every word that comes from the mouth of the LORD" (see Deuteronomy 8:3).

Jesus' experience in the wilderness shows us the presence of fasting in his own life. We find it in his teaching during the Sermon on the Mount. There, he says to his hearers,

> "When you fast, do not look gloomy like the hypocrites, for they disfigure their faces that their fasting may be seen by others. Truly, I say to you, they have received their reward. But when you fast, anoint your head and wash your face, that your fasting may not be seen by others but by your

Father who is in secret. And your Father who sees in secret will reward you." (Matt. 6:16–18)

At times, Jesus could be criticized by the Pharisees and even by the disciples of John the Baptist because it didn't seem to them as if his own disciples fasted at all.[5] How to reconcile those encounters with his clear teaching about fasting in the Sermon on the Mount is not quite clear. It is possible that Jesus' responses to his questioners in each instance were meant to impart the lesson he wanted them to have at that time. As he did at other times, Jesus refused to be drawn into debate on the terms posed by those who were trying to put him on the spot. He didn't feel the need to explain that his followers fasted quietly and without great show, and with that attitude his responses embodied the same humility that he wanted his disciples to embrace when they fasted themselves.

Fasting in Wesleyan Spirituality

Two points about John Wesley's view on fasting show us how important he believed this spiritual practice was as a means of grace. One is that he was deeply frustrated that it seemed to him as if almost no one in his context understood fasting very well. In a sermon on fasting in the New Testament, Wesley argues that fasting is the one means of grace that is the most misunderstood. Some people overvalue its worth, fasting to the point of doing serious damage to their health. Others neglect it entirely, as if it has no importance whatsoever. "It is not all; nor yet is it nothing," Wesley explains. "It is not the end; but it is a precious means thereto, a means which God himself has ordained; and in which therefore, when it is duly used, he will surely give us his blessing."[6] The key is to take fasting seriously but to fast in moderation. When people respond to his encouragements about fasting by saying that they cannot fast at all for fear of hurting their health, he responds wisely as a good pastor should. Rather than abstaining entirely from food, such people should abstain from luxuries: coffee, tea, chocolate, and the like. And even if they don't feel they should abstain from meals entirely, Wesley reasons, they can eat lighter meals and forsake certain types of food for periods of time (such as meat).[7] In other words, there are multiple ways to fast and any single person should only fast in a way that makes sense for him or her. The point is not to earn merit; it is to humble yourself before God and seek to be filled with his Holy Spirit.

"And with fasting let us always join fervent prayer, pouring out our whole souls before God, confessing our sins with all their aggravations, humbling ourselves under his mighty hand, laying open before him all our wants, all our guiltiness and helplessness."

—John Wesley[8]

The second point Wesley makes about fasting is that fasting is often connected with other spiritual disciplines in the Bible. Fasting and prayer are often coupled together: that is true in the Sermon on the Mount itself, and it is also true of the ministry of the apostles in the book of Acts.[9] This is enough for Wesley to encourage strongly that we should go about the Christian life with "earnest prayer and fasting."

The former draws us near to God so that we might be met by his Spirit, while the latter seeks to empty us so that we might be filled again with grace.

Along with combining fasting with prayer, Wesley also sees fasting as connected with what he calls the "works of mercy." These are activities he identifies with Jesus' teaching to feed the hungry, clothe the naked, visit the sick and imprisoned, and welcome the stranger. (We'll look at the works of mercy more fully in Chapter 9.) When it comes to their connection to fasting, the prophet Isaiah in the Old Testament points the way:

> Is not this the fast that I choose:
>   to loose the bonds of wickedness,
>   to undo the straps of the yoke,
> to let the oppressed go free,
>   and to break every yoke?
> Is it not to share your bread with the hungry
>   and bring the homeless poor into your house;
> when you see the naked, to cover him,
>   and not to hide yourself from your own flesh?
> Then shall your light break forth like the dawn,
>   and your healing shall spring up speedily;
> your righteousness shall go before you;
>   the glory of the LORD shall be your rear guard.
>   (Isa. 58:6–8)

It's an absolutely arresting passage in Isaiah. To link the idea of a fast with the ministries of mercy described in this passage suggests that we learn something central about the love of God when we put aside our own grand plans and objectives in order to pursue God's desires for the welfare of his children.[10]

The spiritual benefits of fasting are clear enough in the biblical witness: repentance, humility, mourning, intercession, and an aid to prayer. In the Wesleyan view, all that is left is for us to trust God enough to believe that fasting will be a means of grace in our lives. "Do you know the obligation and the benefit of fasting? How often do you practice it?" Wesley asks us. "The neglect of this alone is sufficient to account for our feebleness and faintness of spirit. We are continually grieving the Holy Spirit of God by the habitual neglect of a plain duty! Let us amend from this hour."[11] Given that fasting is as rare in our day as it was in Wesley's own, that is sound advice.

Fasting in Our Daily Discipleship

It may be the case that there is no spiritual practice more at odds with our present culture than fasting. We live in an era when we are taught to expect that we can get anything we want, whenever we want. By and large, we don't even have to leave the comfort of our own homes in the process. It's all just a mouse click away! Any felt need can be satisfied through a Google search and a credit card purchase. Pretty much anything you desire you can have delivered right to your doorstep, two-day shipping available.

So what does it mean to suggest that doing just the opposite of what the culture encourages could actually be one of the most important things we can do in our lives? "Hello there, Mr. Consumer. I know everything you hear or read from television, radio, and the Internet says you should indulge every appetite you have. But I'm here to tell you that actually denying yourself to the point of physical discomfort could be the very means that God will use to

transform your life!" It sounds crazy. Bizarrely countercultural. It's the sort of thing that would surely make the list of
"least popular things that Christians do."

I'll admit that the practice of fasting has never been easy
for me. Until recently, my attempts to fast were limited to
the season of Lent. At the onset of Lent each year, I commit
to abstaining from something I sincerely enjoy (usually a
type of food) although even there I find myself breaking
my fast at some point during Lent more often than not. The
approach to fasting that I have embraced more recently is
a Friday fast—from waking till three o'clock in the afternoon (although sometimes I'll shorten it to noon on days
when I have a speaking engagement and have to have a
sharp mind). The Friday fast is something I've come to look
forward to, and it does help to center me inwardly on God.

I actually think that it is the very countercultural nature
of fasting that can make it a powerful means of grace in the
present. Christians used to speak positively about the spiritual value of suffering. As we became more sensitive to how
that message can come across to victims of child or spousal
abuse, we have tended to shy away from the "suffering is
good for you" message. But surely there is a certain type
of voluntary suffering that can have real spiritual benefit.
That is particularly the case in a consumerist culture. We
have abundance all around us to the point that most of us
are guilty of gluttony to some degree. Taking the step of
saying that we will deny ourselves food so that we can be
filled with the Holy Spirit could be a practice that serves to
jar us out of the worst of our consumerist idolatries.

The way we could go about applying fasting to our daily
discipleship might take on a number of different forms.
Adopting fasting as a Lenten discipline in the period before

Easter is not a bad way to start. From personal experience, I can say that a weekly Friday fast can be a beginning point as well (and one that isn't limited to a specific season of the year). For people who just have a hard time fasting in general, taking Wesley's advice might be the way to go: choose a particular food or beverage that you love or rely upon, and abstain from it one or two days each week as a partial fast. Beyond these options, I'd simply say that our motivation for fasting really does make a difference. If you want to go on a diet for your appearance or health, then go on a diet. We don't fast to lose weight; we fast so that we can be drawn closer to Christ Jesus.

Since fasting does involve denying yourself true bodily necessities, we should also be wise in the way we go about it. People with medical conditions that cause them to need to eat certain types of food at certain specific times may have to accept that this means of grace is simply not available to them. For the rest of us, though, we should make some serious attempt to embrace a practice of moderate fasting. Better yet, do it together with a spouse, a friend, or with fellow members of a small group. Both the encouragement and the accountability will be helpful.

Not long ago, I heard a sermon that dealt with fasting as a major topic. It occurred to me afterward that it was probably the first sermon on fasting I'd ever heard. The preacher connected fasting with self-control. He said, "Fasting is a way of saying, 'I will not be controlled by my appetites. I will not be controlled by the external forces in the world around me.'"[12] This strikes me as a very timely message for us today. After all, we are all surrounded by idols. They may not look like carved statues or totem poles anymore, but they are things that compete for our

allegiance just the same: our possessions, wealth, technological devices, and cravings for entertainment or sex or
food. These things will rule our lives if we let them and they
are always around us.

We begin to make headway against them when
we realize that discipleship is akin to athletic training.
And as any serious athlete can tell you, becoming excellent in one sport or another takes a lot of discipline and,
yes, self-control. "The positive side of self-control," the
preacher said that Sunday, "is that we are all called to be
spiritual athletes." It's no coincidence that the apostle
Paul talks about fighting the good fight and running the
race in conjunction with keeping the faith. Nor should it
surprise us that Hebrews tells us to run with perseverance
the race that is set before us. Athletic training can transform a person's body into something remarkable. Spiritual
training can do the same thing with a person's heart and
soul—and fasting should be a chief component of it.

CHAPTER 7

Fellowship

ONE EVENING IN JULY OF 2001, I STOOD ON A balcony of the Hotel Oasis in Chincha Alta, Peru. I had been in Peru for almost two weeks with a mission team. We were working with the Methodist Church of Peru to build a church and community center to serve the children of a poor outlying area of the city. With me on that balcony were a college student who was serving as our translator and Rev. Pedro Uchuya-Torres, the pastor of the church in Chincha Alta and our host. I knew very little Spanish at that time. We had struggled to communicate over the course of the trip, and the cultural challenges between the American group and the Peruvian host congregation were at least as great as the language difference. Yet Pedro had remained gracious and patient throughout our time with him, and now we were getting ready to say good-bye.

We spoke for a while through our translator. We mostly reflected on what we had accomplished and what was still to be done. Near the end of the conversation, Pedro remarked, "I have learned that the most important gifts we have are not material things, but rather the chance to walk together as brothers despite our differences and to know that we are children of the same Father." I was struck by his words and the wisdom from which they came. Then I replied that I considered myself fortunate to count Pedro and his congregation as my brothers and sisters. Pedro smiled, looked at me, and said, "We're not so far apart."

My friend Pedro showed me something that evening about the fruits of real Christian fellowship. He's shown me much more in the years since, and I am grateful to call him a friend. He is well aware that the fellowship we can share as disciples of Jesus Christ is the most powerful form of community available to us. What surprises me is that so few Christians seem to share Pedro's awareness. Real Christian fellowship is a means of grace, and the promise it holds for us can be summed up with three simple statements about discipleship. First, we can never do it on our own. Second, God doesn't intend for us to do it on our own. And third, when we experience the power of deep Christian fellowship, we find that we would never want to do it on our own.[1]

Christian Fellowship in the Biblical Witness

The biblical story from Genesis to Revelation tells us that we are meant to be together. When God created Adam and placed him in the garden of Eden, it was not long before God said, "It is not good for the man to be alone" (Gen. 2:18 NIV). So God gave Eve to the man to be his wife. From that time onward, the story of the Bible is the story of God's relationship with his people. Israel is not a bunch of loosely connected individuals. Israel is a *people*. And throughout the long history of slavery and redemption, exile and return, we get the distinct sense that the people of Israel are not whole unless all Israel's twelve tribes are together in the land.

When Jesus Christ came into the world, he gave a special meaning to fellowship through the way he carried out his ministry. Jesus called twelve disciples to be with him (an echo of those twelve tribes of Israel). Then he forged them into a community, and that community would become the nucleus of the Christian church.

> "As iron sharpens iron, so one person sharpens another."
> —Proverbs 27:17 NIV

One of the remarkable things about biblical faith is that it is never an individual matter. Israel is a people. God's promise to Abraham was to make of him a great nation. Later, God sent Moses to tell Pharaoh, "Let my people go." Jesus does not counsel individuals one-on-one. He calls twelve disciples to follow him. The word *church* itself means "assembly." The Christian faith is certainly something that is given to individuals, but part of receiving it involves being grafted into a believing community.

Remember the core Scripture passage that gives us our model for the means of grace in the Acts of the Apostles: "They devoted themselves to the apostles' teaching and the fellowship, to the breaking of bread and the prayers" (v. 2:42). Right at the beginning of the church's life, the first Christians understood that their *fellowship* was a part of who they were.

I personally find it remarkable that so many of Jesus' instructions to his disciples are aimed at what it means to live together within a faith community. In his counsel about how to deal with disciplinary problems in the church, Jesus assures us that we can handle disputes and differences in a loving way. The reason for this assurance is simply because Jesus will never leave us: "For where two or three are gathered in my name, I am there among them" (Matt. 18:20 NRSV). Likewise, Jesus makes loving one another the very mark of authentic discipleship. "A new commandment I give to you," he says, "that you love one another: just as I have loved you, you also are to love one another" (John 13:34). It's a high bar, to be sure. He is not saying that we should love one another only when we feel like it, or on our good days. He's rather saying that we should love one another as he has loved us. And that means that we should love one another to the extent that we would be willing to die for one another. Christian fellowship in the biblical sense is no small thing.

Christian Fellowship in Wesleyan Spirituality

Fellowship is last on the list of Wesley's instituted means of grace. This is the one practice of discipleship on his list that is perhaps the least obvious from a biblical point of view. But as we've seen, there is plenty of direct scriptural support for thinking about fellowship as initiated by Jesus to be one of the practices that his followers will pursue as they grow in their discipleship.

One of the most important things to understand about Christian fellowship as a means of grace is that there's a difference between the way that John Wesley uses the word *fellowship* and the way that we tend to use it. When we use fellowship, we use it as a common noun. It's simply what happens when people get together and spend time in one another's company.

Wesley's uses this term in a different way. He uses fellowship almost like a proper noun: Fellowship (instead of fellowship). He has something very specific in mind when he speaks of Christian fellowship, which we can see in places where he is defending the Methodist movement against those in his day who did not understand it.[2]

In fact, the way Wesley defends Methodist evangelism says a lot about what he understands true fellowship to be. There were people in England who wished that Wesley and the other early Methodists would just cease and desist their evangelistic work. They thought that Methodists were disruptive and threatened the Church of England with schism. They wanted the Methodists to let the normal routine of the parish churches in England supply whatever form of religious fellowship was needed. There were plenty of true Christians in the parish churches, these critics argued, and the Methodists' activities were destroying the fellowship they already enjoyed.

Wesley's response is to argue that his critics don't understand the real meaning of fellowship at all. He argues that, prior to the coming of the Methodists, authentic Christian fellowship in many parts of England was entirely absent. To those who claimed that Methodists destroyed the fellowship of the parish churches, Wesley's reply is blunt: "That which never existed cannot be destroyed," he says. Then he goes on to describe the character of the fellowship that he is talking about:

> Which of those true Christians had any such fellowship with these [i.e., the false Christians who make up the majority of parish congregations]?

Who watched over them in love? Who marked their growth in grace? Who advised and exhorted them from time to time? Who prayed with them and for them as they had need? This, and this alone is Christian fellowship.[3]

The irony that his opponents don't want to admit, according to Wesley, is that the very opposite of what they are claiming is the truth. Whatever real fellowship might have existed in local parish churches has been killed by spiritual deadness. And in that kind of a situation, Methodist evangelistic work ought to be welcomed with open arms. "What a mere jest is it, then, to talk so gravely of *destroying* what never was!" Wesley says. "The real truth is just the reverse of this: we *introduce* Christian fellowship where it was *utterly destroyed*. And the fruits of it have been peace, joy, love, and zeal for every good word and work."[4] So not only does real fellowship have a particular (and active!) sort of meaning, but it can also be measured by a biblical standard. Where it occurs, it will produce fruits of the spirit like love, joy, peace, and all the rest.

There's also a phrase in the quotation above that was very important to Wesley's view of what fellowship was really about: *to watch over one another in love*. It means that fellowship is not just about getting together to pass the time. It's also not about getting together for purposes of entertainment. There's a deeply spiritual component to fellowship, in Wesley's mind, that makes it centrally about the work of transformation. This was something that he actually saw happen again and again. He reported such occurrences in the journal that he published for others to read. In one entry from the year 1780, Wesley describes a gathering of Methodists in the area of Warrington right after Easter: "The next evening, when a few of the society were met together, the power of God came mightily upon them. Some fell to the ground, some cried aloud for mercy, some rejoiced with joy unspeakable. Two or three found a clear sense of the love of God . . ." Of those who had a direct experience of God's love, Wesley describes one "young woman in particular, who was lately much prejudiced against [the Methodist] way but is now filled with joy unspeakable."[5] The kinds of experience that the one at Warrington reflects could come in a variety of settings— prayer gatherings, preaching services, and love feasts. The key element that was common in each of them was that Christian believers were gathered together with their hearts open to the work of the Holy Spirit and with a desire to receive God's grace.

The other word that Wesley uses to describe Christian fellowship is *conference*. That's a term we usually associate with meetings held at convention centers. But for Wesley, the idea of conference is rooted in the verb *to confer*. Christian conference in this sense is about believers coming together to focus on their faith: to pray, to share their experience of God, to seek advice and to offer counsel, and even to confess their sins and ask for forgiveness.

When fellowship takes the form of conferencing between Christians, it comes in the kind of small group discipleship settings that the early Methodist movement was built upon. The two primary such groups were the band meeting and the class meeting. When he was explaining the effects of the class meeting, in particular, Wesley wrote:

> Many now happily experienced that Christian fellowship of which they had not so much as an idea before. They began to "bear one another's

burdens," and "naturally" to "care for each other."
As they had daily a more intimate acquaintance
with, so they had a more endeared affection for
each other. And "speaking the truth in love, they
grew up into him in all things which is the head,
even Christ."[6]

A testimony like that
makes clear the depth of what
Wesley means by conference.
It takes hard work to get to
this level. Real commitment
which extends over time is
a necessity. A great deal of
honesty and trust is required
as well. For a small group of
committed believers who are
willing to join together with
such a common purpose,
though, the spiritual growth
they experience together can
be remarkable.

> "Christian
> conference: Are
> you convinced how
> important and how
> difficult it is to 'order
> your conversation
> right'? Is it always
> in grace? Seasoned
> with salt? Meet to
> minister grace to the
> hearers?"
>
> —John Wesley

Christian Fellowship in Our Daily Discipleship

Where have you learned the most profound lessons of your
life? How have you been shaped in the deepest ways? What
are the events and experiences that come to mind when
you think about these things?

If you are like me, then you will think about teachers,
family members, and friends. You think about relationships.

And you think about specific moments and happenings when a conversation with someone else had a real impact on your life. When we talk about Christian fellowship as a means of grace, we are talking about how we grow spiritually through our relationships and experiences with other followers of Jesus. It can be pretty countercultural to double down on the need for disciplined community in our lives today. Our society is the most hyper-individualistic that has ever existed on earth. We receive constant messages that what is most important is our own felt sense of happiness. (And *happiness* in this sense usually means something that we can buy or an entertainment that we can experience to relieve our boredom.)

A community to which we are beholden, on the other hand, is an intrusion on the very idea of individualistic gratification. The community can tell you what is good for you. And the community can tell you what you should not be doing as well. If you believe that you are responsible for the well-being of others in a community, that will constrain your freedom. Sometimes you will have to act for the good of others in a way that denies what you might want to do for yourself.

Does our culture even allow for such an ideal to be practiced anymore? Can we truly grapple with the notion that the most flourishing form of life is a life where we say "no" to ourselves so that we can say "yes" to a greater good? Is it still possible for us to find our core identity in relationship rather than in the claim to be an autonomous self?

I think the challenges to all of this are great. I also think that nothing less than the Christian faith is at stake. Today, people think nothing of church-hopping the same way that they hop from fast-food restaurant to fast-food restaurant, just to satisfy a passing whim. Church has become like an entry on a to-do list, which often has no more priority than soccer practice, a favorite television show, or the laundry. A pastor friend once told me that he got increasingly frustrated at his church members' responses to his statement, "We missed you at church last Sunday." The responses themselves were fairly understandable: "Oh, we went out of town to see the ballgame," or "We were visiting our grandkids," or "We were at the beach." So finally, my friend began asking a follow-up: "Oh! That's great. Which church did you visit while you were there?" He wasn't necessarily trying to put people on the spot. He was simply trying to get across the message that worship on Sundays should be the number-one priority of all Christians, no matter where they happen to be. The trend even amongst churchgoing Christians seems to be either that church is an option people will choose when they have nothing better to do, or else that church is a burdensome duty that trips out of town allow them to escape.

What if the reality is something quite different? What if church is simply the community where we find salvation? After all, salvation is not something that we are given like a magic token to possess outright. Salvation comes in the form of a relationship. It is a relationship with Jesus Christ, and Jesus is the one who tells us in very particular terms that he is calling us into a community of faith. So if we reject the community that he calls us into, it might just tell us something about whether we really care anything about knowing him after all. There is no loving God apart from loving neighbor, and loving neighbor is a concrete thing that takes place first and foremost within the fellowship of Christian believers.[7]

I have tried to be a part of a covenant group everywhere I've lived since I started seminary more than fifteen years ago. Right now, that group is made up of eight people in our church who meet weekly to pray, share how they have experienced God, and take counsel from one another about what is going on in our lives. It works, because we have been committed to one another for a long time and we trust one another. After we had been together for about a year, I asked whether or not everyone in the group wanted to continue. (I felt like I needed to do that, since I had not asked for a multiyear commitment on the front end.) The other members of the group acted surprised that I would even raise the question. One woman who had never been a part of a small group before said, "I don't want to stop doing this at all. This is the most important thing that's ever happened in my spiritual life."

Now I don't want to romanticize what our covenant group is like. We have our ups and downs, like all such groups. There are some weeks were we dig into deep and rich spiritual material, and there are other weeks where we have a hard time getting below the surface level. Our persistence and commitment to one another have borne fruit in all of our lives, though, and through our group's life we have learned something very real about power of Christian fellowship as a means of grace.

Like most things worth doing in life, embracing true Christian fellowship takes a serious commitment. The good news is that the commitment is worth it. But since fellowship involves a community of people, our commitment will have to be made in concert with others. All of us have been shaped to think like consumers. Unfortunately, consumer choices are all about me, my, and mine. If we want to take fellowship (or conference) as a central part of our discipleship in the Wesleyan sense, we will have to begin making new choices. Those choices are not choices we can make our own. We'll have to make them within—that's right—a community. And we have to be committed to that community entirely. There is no dabbling in real discipleship.

PART II

What We Learn from Our Context:

The Prudential Means of Grace

"Then the King will say to those on his right, 'Come, you who are blessed by my Father, inherit the kingdom prepared for you from the foundation of the world. For I was hungry and you gave me food, I was thirsty and you gave me drink, I was a stranger and you welcomed me, I was naked and you clothed me, I was sick and you visited me, I was in prison and you came to me.'"

—Matthew 25:34–36

CHAPTER 8

Classes, Bands, and Arts of Holy Living

HAVE YOU EVER HAD AN EXPERIENCE THAT WAS many times more powerful than you thought it would be? Or maybe an encounter that affected you in a way you just never anticipated? When that's happened to me, it has usually been when I've encountered something extraordinary. Climbing to the top of Mount Sinai with a group of pilgrims in time to watch the sun go down was one for me. Witnessing the birth of my first child was another. Sometimes life experiences can be the means for unexpected grace.

When you think about it, this very feature of our lives suggests something about the means of grace. We know that the instituted means of grace are real means of grace because they've been instituted (or put in place) by Jesus Christ. But we also discover other things to be means of grace, not because they are commanded by God but because the *experience* of them conveys spiritual power to us. Sometimes these are extraordinary happenings—as with the birth of a child or some other monumental event. Yet while these extraordinary experiences of life are wonderful, we have to receive them simply as rare and treasured gifts. (After all, that's what makes them extraordinary. They don't come around all the time.) The good news is that we also find that some quite ordinary experiences of daily life can be means of grace as well. These are habits or practices that we embrace exactly because of the spiritual benefit they offer. The great thing about such ordinary practices is that we *can* indeed count on them in day-to-day life. These are what we call the prudential means of grace.

The word *prudence* means practical wisdom. Prudence is the kind of wisdom you gain through maturity and the experience of daily life. When you use prudence as a Christian to look at how your discipleship is exercised in the course of daily living, you begin to see how certain things act as spurs to your own spiritual growth. Those things will always lie in harmony with Jesus' two great commandments—to love the Lord our God and to love your neighbor as yourself. Beyond that, though, they will likely be shaped by your own context. Our discipleship must be carried out in the twenty-first century, because that is when we live. We don't live in first-century Israel or eighteenth-century England. By using our practical wisdom, we can discover the sorts of contemporary discipleship practices that will serve as true means of grace in our own day.

The Wesleyan Basis for the Prudential Means of Grace

John Wesley was devoted to practicing the instituted means of grace as a fundamental part of his discipleship. He was a creative and practical leader, though, and that meant that he was open to new ideas for how to live the Christian life. One of the things that Wesley realized early on was that *context* makes a real difference in how the Christian life is lived. Think about the vast cultural and technological changes that separate us from Wesley's eighteenth-century world. Then think about the even greater differences that separate us from the time and culture when Jesus lived. There are all sorts of particular things about our context that we need to take into account when we think about how to live faithfully as Christian people.[1]

When Wesley was working out his views on the means of grace, he developed the category of prudential means of grace as a companion to the instituted means of grace. He believed that recognizing newer practices of discipleship relevant to his own context as means of grace was important. The way that he described the prudential means of grace early in his life was like this:

> Whatever I know to do me hurt, that to me is not
>   indifferent, but resolutely to be abstained from;
> Whatever I know to do me good, that to me is not
>   indifferent, but resolutely to be embraced.[2]

He's saying that there is a certain flexibility to how we can understand this category of the means of grace. The spiritual substance of the means of grace is the same no matter how we classify them—it is God's grace at work in us! What differs is the form that some of the means of grace take. And this is because the particular ways in which Christians live out their faith can often be contingent upon the times and circumstances in which they live. By using our prudence—the practical wisdom that comes from experience—we come to know what is spiritually beneficial to us. And that means that the idea of the prudential means of grace is very important.

Generally speaking, Wesley emphasized the prudential means of grace in three areas: particular rules for personal discipleship, small group fellowship, and the works of mercy. We'll look at the first two of these in this chapter, and then we will take up the works of mercy in the next.

Particular Rules and Arts of Holy Living

Early on in his life, John Wesley embraced habits meant to provide a pattern for how to use every hour of his day well. He called this "redeeming the time," and it was intended to help him use every moment God gave him on earth in the most faithful way possible. It's really an impressive approach to life when you think about it, even if it made Wesley both obsessive and anxious about his spiritual state. While he eventually let go of many of those early practices, there was one thing that he became convinced about at a relatively young age: a belief in the value of applying rules to guide your daily discipleship.

Now it's true that some Christians will hear a word like "rules" and get very nervous. Isn't that some form of legalism? When we start to think that the Christian faith is really about following certain rules, aren't we heading toward works righteousness? Actually, that isn't the way that Wesley used rules at all. He used them as healthy guidelines to keep him on the right track. Eventually he even became convinced that a set of rules was needed to keep all Methodist folk under his leadership on the right track. These came to be called the "General Rules," and for many years adhering to them was a requirement to belong to a Methodist society.

Why use rules? Actually the reason for using a set of rules as the guidelines for your life is as relevant now as it was then. Simply put, we are creatures of habit. We are going to follow one routine or another. If we don't make some intentional commitments about what that routine will be, then our life circumstances will dictate it for us. For some people, routine is determined by a job. For others, it might be determined by a favorite hobby or form of entertainment. Addicts have their routines determined by their drug of choice. Many people nowadays are so caught in the grip of social media that their routines are set by how they use their smart phones, laptops, and tablet computers.

The question to ask is whether the routine into which you have fallen makes you truly happy. If you believe that Saint Augustine was right when he prayed to God, "Our hearts are restless until they rest in thee," then you've got to at least consider that the only true happiness is the happiness we know in Jesus Christ when we grow in our faith and learn what it means to be mature disciples. Since habits are hard to break, the bad ones we have won't be undone simply by resolving to stop doing them. Instead, we need to have something to put in their place. And that's where rules (in the Wesleyan sense) come into play.

In one place where Wesley is explaining the prudential means of grace, he starts by asking a couple of questions: "What particular rules have you in order to grow in grace? What arts of holy living?" I love that phrase—*arts of holy living*—because I think it puts the idea of rules in the right context. We are all different from one another in many ways, and what is spiritually helpful to me might not be spiritually helpful to you. What is true of every single one of us, though, is that we will struggle to integrate our discipleship into every aspect of our lives if we don't work at it. So one way to think about how certain rules would be helpful to you is to think about rules as arts of holy living that draw you closer to Christ each day.

I have a friend named Jeff who is a runner, and his daily practice is to get up before the sun and go on a run while the rest of our town is still asleep. I've heard him speak convincingly about the way that his mind and heart are drawn to God on his daily runs. As he works into the rhythm of his stride, he can hear the birds beginning to chirp in the trees of his neighborhood and see the light of the rosy-fingered dawn begin to emerge in the eastern sky. For him, it is more than just a way to keep healthy; it's also a way to be reminded every morning of the goodness of God and the beauty of God's creation. Running, for Jeff, has become an art of holy living.

> "What particular rules have you in order to grow in grace? What arts of holy living?"
>
> —John Wesley

Beyond the particular rules that a person might develop for himself, there was in Wesley's ministry that little matter of the General Rules that were applied to all Methodists. The General Rules were first published in 1743 as a way to bring some discipline to an unruly society of Methodists in the city of Newcastle. There were three rules. Wesley believed that all Christians who were even remotely serious about salvation would reflect a desire to live the right way in their daily lives in certain ways, which he summarized as . . .

> *First*, By doing no harm, by avoiding evil in every kind—especially that which is most generally practiced.

Secondly, By doing good, by being in every kind merciful after their power, as they have opportunity doing good of every possible sort and as far as is possible to all men.

Thirdly, by attending upon all the ordinances of God.[3]

The first thing to note is that the third rule—attending upon all the ordinances of God—is really about the instituted means of grace. In fact, "ordinances of God" is nothing more than a synonym for "instituted means of grace" in Wesley's writing. But what about those first two rules? What about the rule about "doing no harm" and the rule about "doing good" in every possible way?

If you look back on that earlier quotation where Wesley talks about "whatever I know to do me hurt" and "whatever I know to do me good," then it becomes clear that these first two rules are really about the prudential means of grace! And indeed, Wesley offers plenty of practical examples about doing no harm and doing good in the original text of the General Rules. Some of his examples are straight out of Scripture, such as the Golden Rule to do unto others as you would have them do unto you. Other examples are so closely tied to Wesley's context that they can seem quaint to us today. (A later edition of the rules instructed women to avoid wearing "enormous bonnets".) But the point he is making in listing specific examples under each of the rules is important. It's Wesley's way of telling us that these rules are concrete and have a claim on every aspect of our daily lives when we take them seriously. Doing no harm and doing good are more than just nice ideas, in other words. They are guidelines for discipleship, and they are means of grace as well.

Small Group Fellowship: Classes and Bands

One of the most well-known things about the early Methodist movement under John Wesley's leadership is the prominent role that certain types of small group fellowship played. There were a number of these groups, but the two most common were the class meeting and the band meeting. "Never omit meeting your class or band," Wesley writes. "These are the very sinews of our Society; and whatever weakens, or tends to weaken, our regard for these . . . strikes at the very root of our community."[4] It's no exaggeration to say that a great part of the reason that the Methodist movement was so effective was because disciplined small group fellowship lay at the very heart of it.

So what did these classes and bands look like? Class meetings were mandatory for all Methodists in the sense that anyone who wanted to belong to a Methodist society had to belong to a class. The class meeting originally had anywhere from twelve to thirty people in it, and its membership was mixed in terms of men and women. One individual was designated as the class leader and had the responsibility to gather the class every week and ask each member some version of the question, "How goes it with your soul?"[5] This question provided an opportunity for personal testimony, sometimes to celebrate successes and sometimes to talk about challenges or stumbling blocks encountered. Advice and encouragement was offered all around. The accounts of early class meetings that come down to us today demonstrate that it could be a dynamic gathering. People were moved to intense prayer, and newcomers to the class often experienced profound spiritual renewal.

The band meeting had some differences from the class. It was always a voluntary type of group, and it was segregated by gender and marital status. It was also considerably smaller in number, with about three to six people in each band.[6] The band meeting went beyond testimony and faith sharing to focusing more particularly on the mutual confession of sin. This meant that it required more from its members—more commitment, more vulnerability, and more trust. Yet it was also often the setting for even greater levels of spiritual growth.

Wesley's commitment to the use of small group types of fellowship shows us a very creative use of the prudential means of grace. Remember that Christian conference is actually an *instituted* means of grace. *Conference* in the Wesleyan sense of that word is exactly what was going on in class and band meetings. But classes and bands were *prudential* developments in early Methodism, in that they were products of the particular social context of eighteenth-century Britain. Methodist leaders like Wesley saw the good that could come from a gathering like the class or band, and they embraced them wholeheartedly. Nowhere in the Bible does God say, "Go and form class meetings," but that didn't stop the early Methodists from using them as real means of grace.

> "How dare any man deny this to be (as to the substance of it) a means of grace, ordained by God?"
> —John Wesley[7]

Even in those later periods when small group fellowship hasn't been a huge part of Wesleyan spirituality in Methodist circles, there has still been a residual sense that this is where real spiritual growth happens. I was reading through some older church manuals on spiritual formation from the mid-twentieth century, and I came across one with the title *Spiritual Renewal for Methodism*. I was a little surprised at the subtitle: "There Is Redemptive Power in Personal Groups."[8] The book tells the story of the importance of the class meeting in the early Methodist movement. Then it goes on to tell about the class meeting's decline, before making a case for the importance of bringing back a similar practice as a means to revitalize Methodist spirituality in that day. The fact that the little book was published well more than fifty years ago shows that there has always been the memory that small group fellowship was vital to Methodist spirituality. Might this offer us a lesson?

The Prudential Means of Grace in Your Own Life

If context is key when it comes to the prudential means of grace, that means the list could be open-ended. Wesley himself recognized that, and he spoke about the possibility of "multiplying prudential means upon ourselves" as we discover new practices that are particularly effective at promoting our spiritual growth.[9] If we want to think about what the prudential means of grace look like in our context, we would need to identify the discipleship practices we find to be most effective in our lives. A student of mine who is a recovering alcoholic once spoke very passionately in class about how a 12-step recovery program like Alcoholics Anonymous is a true prudential means of grace. I think she was absolutely correct. Indeed, 12-step recovery programs are means of grace that save people's lives every day. I had another student who was very talented musically, and he once explained the way that he finds hymn-singing and praise music to be one of the most powerful means of grace in his own life. For what it's worth, I can personally say that I've found the covenant groups to which I belonged over the years to be extremely important means of grace in my life. (These small groups have usually operated in similar ways to early Methodist band meetings.)

Now turn the focus to yourself. What discipleship practices are present in your life that you might call prudential means of grace? Being intentional about identifying them as such is an important first step. When you volunteer regularly at your church's soup kitchen, or work in a youth mentoring program, or sing in the chancel choir, these are more than just good works or duties. When approached in the right way and with an open heart, they are true means of grace.

After recognizing that a whole variety of discipleship practices can be seen as authentic means of grace, the second step is asking yourself whether you practice them in a truly disciplined way. The means of grace work on us kind of like practicing free throws works on a basketball player. The basketball player becomes a better free-throw shooter through regular practice, as the motion of lifting the ball and releasing the shot toward the rim, over and over again, gets ingrained into his muscle memory. A former student of mine once said that

> Our practice of the means of grace over time allows grace to wear grooves into our souls.

she thought the way the means of grace work is that, over time, our practice of them allows grace to wear grooves into our souls.[10] I think that's a fantastic way to think about it—and it's also a description that emphasizes the need for discipline in how we practice our faith.

CHAPTER 9

Works of Mercy

RULES FOR HOLY LIVING AND THE CLASS AND band meetings are two of the major examples of the prudential means of grace. Yet there is another example which was central to Wesley's own sense of vital discipleship. Works of mercy, as he called them, are those means of grace that direct Christians outward to people in the world who suffer from spiritual or bodily needs. In a sermon on the importance of visiting the sick, Wesley writes, "Surely there are works of mercy . . . which are real means of grace." And he takes as his foundation for this view the teaching of the apostle Paul in his Letter to the Ephesians: "For we are his workmanship, created in Christ Jesus for good works, which God prepared beforehand, that we should walk in them" (Eph. 2:10).[1] As we are drawn close to Christ in faith, we are called to do the work of Christ in ministering to the poor, the downtrodden, and the outcast. This is God's desire for all those who have been born again through grace. Such a gospel form of living is part of what it means to "walk in newness of life," so how could it be anything other than a powerful means of grace?

What are these works of mercy, specifically? And how exactly do they become means of grace for us in our daily living? These are important questions. Answering them will help us to see even more clearly how the prudential means of grace are central to our spiritual formation as mature disciples of Jesus Christ. Hopefully, we can also see how the means of grace push us to be more outwardly focused and missional in the way we think about the church on the whole.

Biblical Teaching and Common-Sense Reasoning

At times the Methodist movement would experience growing pains as it adapted to changing circumstances in its early years. People at the time didn't like change any more than people do now! So it wasn't uncommon for John Wesley and other Methodist leaders to get pushback whenever new activities and practices were being tried out. For things considered to be among the prudential means of grace, there was less direct scriptural support—and this could lead to objections. Wesley was no shrinking violet, though, and he also tended to think things through in a thorough way. When it came to encouraging new practices that Wesley believed could be effective means of grace, he was ready to answer the inevitable questions that arose.

One of Wesley's responses to some objections that came up in the late 1740s tells us a lot about his flexibility when it came to considering new discipleship practices. It also gives us some insight into the prudential means of grace themselves. It's true, Wesley admits, that there are "these little prudential helps we are continually changing, one thing after another." The experimental element of that approach is not a weakness though, Wesley says. It's rather "a peculiar advantage which we enjoy." True, such practices are "merely prudential, not essential, not of divine institution." But that doesn't mean they aren't spiritually beneficial. It just means that Methodist discipleship has the ability to flex and pivot as needed when new opportunities arise. Wesley says, "We're always open to instruction, willing to be wiser every day than we were before, and to change whatever we can change for the better."[2] If we hear a lot of language today about the need to search out "best practices" in business or education or the church, then it's pretty interesting to find John Wesley himself using that same idea more than 250 years ago.

But wait—it's possible to be so flexible that everything ends up falling apart. We need a solid foundation for our discipleship that we can count on. Talk of finding new "little prudential helps" is good as far as it goes, but how do we ensure that such helps are recognizably Christian?

> "[Prudential means of grace] are methods which men have found, by reason and common sense, for the more effectually applying several scriptural rules, couched in general terms, to particular occasions."
> —John Wesley[3]

It's here that you realize how much Wesley is trying to strike a balance between biblical orthodoxy and missional flexibility. He isn't actually open to every possibility that pops up. The key is in how we go about reading the Bible. Is it the case that the only acceptable Christian practices are those that are specifically laid out in detail somewhere in the biblical text? Or is it rather that Scripture can also point to more general areas of concern for Christian discipleship and then leave it up to us to figure out how those apply in our own day and age?

Wesley's approach to this issue is very much along the lines of the second option. His reasoning is that "the Scripture, in most points, gives only *general* rules, and leaves the *particular* circumstances to be adjusted by the common sense of mankind." How we go about determining the best way to apply the general teachings of Scripture is through the minds and hearts that God has given us. Or, as Wesley puts it, biblical application can be "determined by reason and experience."[4]

I think there is a freeing quality to this sort of practical thinking. It means that we can take general biblical commands—loving our neighbor, making disciples, and doing good to all people—and apply them to our own contexts, all while being assured that such creative ministry can serve as a true means of grace when it is undertaken with a faithful attitude.

Meeting Jesus in the Works of Mercy

So how do the works of mercy fit into this prudential approach to discipleship? It turns out that the works of mercy present us with a great example of the Bible giving us general rules and leaving the particular circumstances up to us. It comes from Matthew 25:31–40, which is a passage that Wesley cites almost every time he talks about works of mercy. The heart of the passage goes like this:

> "When the Son of Man comes in his glory . . . he will separate people one from another as a shepherd

separates the sheep from the goats. And he will place the sheep on his right, but the goats on the left. Then the King will say to those on his right, 'Come, you who are blessed by my Father, inherit the kingdom prepared for you from the foundation of the world. For I was hungry and you gave me food, I was thirsty and you gave me drink, I was a stranger and you welcomed me, I was naked and you clothed me, I was sick and you visited me, I was in prison and you came to me.' Then the righteous will answer him, saying, 'Lord, when did we see you hungry and feed you, or thirsty and give you drink? And when did we see you a stranger and welcome you, or naked and clothe you? And when did we see you sick or in prison and visit you?' And the King will answer them, 'Truly I say to you, as you did it to one of the least of these my brothers, you did it to me.'"

Have you ever thought about how radical that Scripture passage appears when you just read it in a straightforward way? Jesus is telling us that he will meet us in the hungry, the sick, the imprisoned, and the stranger. He calls us to treat such people as if they were the Son of God himself.

If works of piety like prayer, searching the Scriptures, and the Lord's Supper teach us how to love God better, then these works of mercy teach us how to love our neighbor.[5] They also show us how to love as Christ loved. We get the Wesleyan view on that in a wonderful letter that John Wesley sent to Miss J. C. March in the year 1775. He encourages Miss March to press on in her faith until she knows by her own experience "all that love of God which passeth all (speculative) knowledge." He then asks her bluntly if she is willing to know how to dedicate her life more and more fully to God. He says,

> And are you willing to know? Then I will tell you how. Go and see the poor and sick in their own poor little hovels. Take up your cross, woman! Remember the faith! Jesus went before you, and will go with you. Put off the gentlewoman; you bear a higher character. You are an heir of God and joint-heir with Christ![6]

Notice in that little passage how Wesley is offering his pastoral counsel in a way that tracks very closely with Matthew 25. For if we really do meet Jesus in the poor and the sick, then Miss March had every reason to believe that Jesus went before her and would be with her every step of the way.

One of the places where Wesley lays out his view of the works of mercy the best is his sermon, "On Visiting the Sick." Wesley explains in that sermon that the work of visitation is a "plain duty" for Christian believers. He also says that the sick are not just those who have a conventional illness and are lying in a hospital bed. Such people are part of who we mean by "the sick," but the sick also consist of anyone in a state of suffering. "I would include all such as are in a state of affliction, whether of mind or body," Wesley says, "whether they are good or bad, whether they fear God or not."[7] That means that he's including pretty much all those categories of people Jesus names in Matthew's Gospel—the hungry, the poor, the ill, the imprisoned, and the stranger. And since Jesus' command is given to all his followers, this means that the works of mercy are meant for all Christians. In other words, it is not just pastors who are called to offer pastoral care!

It's fairly obvious to see how the poor widow or the imprisoned felon would experience a personal visit as a means of grace. I can tell you from my own experience in ministry that most people who find themselves in hospitals, homeless shelters, and prisons welcome visits from others. They need companionship, encouragement, and prayer just as much as anyone else, but they are often in situations where those important parts of human relationships are hard to come by. Where Wesley's teaching on the works of mercy gets really interesting is when he makes the case that the works of mercy are not only means of grace for *those being visited*, but also for *those doing the visiting*. When we visit the sick and the needy, we are moved to thank God for all the blessings that we ourselves enjoy. At the same time, our sense of compassion and our desire to help others are both increased.[8] In that way, the love we share with others is returned to us and works to transform our hearts. In giving, we find that we receive as well.

The Meaning of the Works of Mercy for Us

We don't use the language of "works of mercy" much today. In fact, you may have never heard that term before you read this book. We do use some words that relate, though: missions, outreach ministries, hospital and shut-in visitation, and the like. One way I think a term like works of mercy is helpful to us is that it helps us see how a whole host of different discipleship practices are related to one another. What makes them all similar is that they are all ways we go about loving our neighbor. Given that loving our neighbor is the second of the two great commandments

Jesus gives us, understanding how we can do that in concrete ways is important!

There are a couple of things I think we should focus upon when we reflect on how to incorporate the works of mercy into our daily discipleship. One is that the works of mercy are not just good deeds that we perform out of a sense of duty or to feel good about a job well done. They are meant to be true means of grace, but for them to be that we have to realize that they call for us to enter into relationships with others.

I have been involved in mission work with the Methodist Church in Peru over several years. In that time, I've taken several dozen people from the United States on trips lasting anywhere from ten days to two weeks. We go to help the church there with a variety of projects—most of them involving building or renovating church buildings and community centers. One of the things I've noticed about some of the folks who go on these mission trips is that they seem to want to do the work of mission without ever actually interacting with any of their Peruvian brothers and sisters while they are there. Sometimes this is because of a sense of intimidation about the English/Spanish language barrier. But sometimes it is also because they have interpreted mission work as simply doing good deeds.

The good deeds are important of course, but much more so is the work of building relationships and learning how to love Christians who are different from yourself. The only way for missions or any other work of mercy to act as a means of grace is for love to be shared. For indeed, the love that Christians share with one another is nothing less than a love shared with them first by Jesus Christ: "By this all people will know that you are my disciples," Jesus said, "if you have love for one another" (John 13:35).

The second thing we should focus upon with the works of mercy is that they are *not* an optional part of what it means to follow Jesus. A Christian who sits in her home all day reading her Bible and praying but failing to put her faith into action has missed something very important about living as a disciple. On the other hand, once she does begin to love God by loving others through the works of mercy, she will find that her whole vision of discipleship starts to change. Rebekah Miles puts it in a way that I find very helpful when she writes, "Just as physical exercise promotes the growth of our bodies, works of mercy can promote the growth of our souls. . . .

> "[A]s the love of God naturally leads to works of piety, so the love of our neighbour naturally leads . . . to works of mercy. It inclines us to feed the hungry, to clothe the naked, to visit them that are sick or in prison; to be as eyes to the blind and feet to the lame; a husband to the widow, a father to the fatherless."
>
> —John Wesley[9]

They are, ultimately, both an expression of, and tinder for, the love of God that centers our life."[10] In the Gospels, we find Jesus constantly *sending out* those who gather around him so that his message will reach others through word and deed. For those of us who want to follow Jesus today, we should understand ourselves as sent out as well.

When we recognize that the works of mercy are really about taking the *general rule* to feed the hungry, visit the sick, and welcome the stranger, and applying it to the *specific contexts* of our own lives, we will all of a sudden realize that the list of what makes up a work of mercy is potentially endless. A soup kitchen or food pantry, a Habitat for Humanity home build, a prison ministry, a program of homebound and nursing home visitation, teaching English as a second language, or a mission trip—these are all works of mercy that invite us to share the love of Jesus with our neighbor. The more we share that love, the more we will find the same love returned to us so that it transforms our very lives.

PART III

What We Learn by Contemplation:

The General Means of Grace

"Then Jesus told his disciples, 'If anyone would come after me, let him deny himself and take up his cross and follow me. For whoever would save his life will lose it, but whoever loses his life for my sake will find it.'"

—Matthew 16:24–25

CHAPTER 10

Exercising the Presence of God

UP TO THIS POINT WE'VE LOOKED AT A NUMBER of different means of grace. These are all practices that are more or less familiar to us. We can identify prayer easily enough, and we know what the Lord's Supper looks like in the context of worship. Even if you hadn't practiced some of the means of grace before reading this book, you were probably familiar with the concepts. Do all the means of grace take the form of particular practices, though? Or are there some means of grace that are more about our inner lives—the dispositions of our hearts?

Think for a moment about the difference between doing something where you are just going through the motions and doing something where you put your whole heart into that thing. The difference is huge. We can be talking about the very same activity either way, but your *experience* of that activity is going to be dramatically different depending on your level of attention and commitment. I played football growing up, and I remember how different a football practice could seem depending on whether I wanted to be there or not. If I was tired or hurt, the practice could be miserable. The heat seemed hotter and the drills took longer. But if I was really excited—if I knew that I was going to start in the game that week, or if the team was really coming together with a purpose—then practice could be downright fun. It was all about my inner attitude. When my heart was in it, the whole experience changed.

When it came to the means of grace, John Wesley knew that it was not enough just to talk about the spiritual practices themselves. It wouldn't suffice just to talk about *what* we do. He also needed to talk about *why* we do what we do, and *how* we do what we do. His term for that is the "general means of grace" and it is the subject of this final chapter.

The general means of grace are related to our inward spiritual intention. When God speaks to our hearts, we find that our hearts are given power to yearn for God. We have to pay attention to this yearning, naturally, and we have to focus it toward God. But when we do, this inward spiritual focus then becomes a means of grace itself. It is a *general* means of grace because it affects our whole being. The remarkable thing we'll find is that by affecting us generally, it enables us to experience each of the *particular* means of grace more powerfully.[1]

The Foundation for the Whole Spiritual Life

We can get a pretty good sense about what Wesley means by the general means of grace when we see how he compares this category with the other two we have seen so far—the instituted means of grace and the prudential means of grace. When he is explaining these different types of the means of grace to his preachers, Wesley first lays out the instituted means of grace and gives a list of them. Then he follows that by explaining what he means by the prudential means of grace. And at that point, he says something very interesting. "These means may be used without fruit," Wesley says, and he's talking about both the instituted and prudential means of grace! Essentially, he means that you can use them in such a mechanical way that they give you no spiritual benefit.

This makes sense when you think about it. I can mouth the words of a prayer without thinking much at all about what I am really saying. I can also sit through a sermon watching the preacher the whole time, all while my mind is on what I'm going to eat for lunch that day. I could walk forward to receive the Lord's Supper, with my thoughts preoccupied with how angry I am at a coworker with whom I had an argument the week before. Or I could volunteer to serve meals at the local homeless shelter because it seems like a good thing to do, even though every minute I'm there I am focused judgmentally on how dirty and unkempt the residents of the shelter appear.

In each of these examples, the power that the means of grace might otherwise convey would be nullified by my absentmindedness or hardness of heart. With no inward sense of intention, God's grace will never reach me. For grace to really have an impact on us, we must be open to it. And for the means God has provided to act as channels for that grace, we have to have a desire to meet God in those means! That is Wesley's point by saying that we can *use* all of the instituted and prudential means in a way that makes them *useless*.

Wesley goes on, though, to explain that there are some means which cannot be used without fruit. They are always going to be effective. And he gives a very interesting list of what he's talking about: watching, denying ourselves, taking up our cross, and the exercise of the presence of God.[2] The first three of those terms are all straight out of the Bible. The idea of watching (or keeping spiritually alert) shows up both in the prophets of the Old Testament and in Jesus' teaching in the New Testament. Denying ourselves and taking up our cross also comes from Jesus, where he lists these two things as necessary for anyone who would seek to follow him (Matt. 16:24). The exercise of the presence of God is not a direct quotation from Scripture, but it does appear to be closely related to the theme of God's universal presence that appears in several of the psalms. Psalm 139 says,

> Where shall I go from your Spirit?
> Or where shall I flee from your presence?
> If I ascend to heaven, you are there!
> If I make my bed in Sheol, you are there! (vv. 7–8)

And Psalm 16 says,

> You make known to me the path of life;
> in your presence there is fullness of joy;
> at your right hand are pleasures forevermore. (v. 11)

In both of these examples, the presence of God is depicted as being all around us and available if we will but open the eyes of our heart to receive it. Watching, exercising the presence of God, and the rest are not particular practices in the sense of concrete activities so much as they are ways of being contemplative and intentional about the spiritual life.

Elsewhere, Wesley gives other lists of the general means of grace that are similar to the one I mentioned above. The items on each list are not always identical, but they do all have to do with our inward intentionality. In one listing, he adds universal obedience and keeping all the commandments to denying ourselves and taking up our cross. In another, he treats certain traits of the Beatitudes from the Sermon on the Mount as general means of grace: meekness, hungering and thirsting after righteousness, being merciful, and being pure in heart.

Hungering and thirsting after righteousness is a good example to use because the parallel between it and hungering and thirsting after food and drink is so plain. The Scripture passage comes from Matthew 5:6, which reads, "Blessed are those who hunger and thirst for righteousness, for they shall be satisfied." Hunger and thirst are "the strongest of all our bodily appetites," Wesley explains. We never go a day without eating food and drinking water if we can help it. The craving for both will drive us to distraction if we go without them for just a few hours. "In like manner," Wesley says, "this hunger in the soul, this thirst after the image of God, is the strongest of all our spiritual appetites when it is once awakened in the heart."[3] When we don't try to numb our hunger for God with other things, we'll have the inward desire to know and love God that will make us ready for his grace.

So the general means of grace are all about the inward dispositions of the heart. One of Wesley's favored phrases to describe the true meaning of the Christian life is that it is expressed through "holiness of heart and life." And get this: he never, ever reverses the order of those two. It is *always* holiness of heart and life and *never* holiness of life and heart. The reason is that he believes the inner nature of the heart will always end up ruling the outer actions of

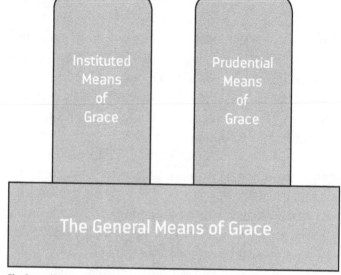

The General Means of Grace serve as the foundation for all the other means of grace. When our hearts are attuned to God, we find that all those things we do in Christ's name become spiritually transformative for us.

life. If you have a wicked heart or a lazy heart or a greedy heart, then eventually your life is going to be lived wickedly, slothfully, or avariciously. On the other hand, if you have a gentle heart, you will be a gentle person in your outward living. If you have a loving heart, then you will show love in all areas of your life. There's a connection between this idea and how the general means of grace relate to all the other means of grace. Whether you want to call it being watchful, or being universally obedient, or exercising the presence of God, in the end all of those terms refer in some way to having the inward disposition to know and love God. Someone whose soul is accurately described by those terms is ready and willing to be transformed by Jesus Christ! And that results in the means of grace that look like practices of discipleship (the instituted and prudential) that will be spiritually effective when they are used. Because of this relationship between the various categories of the means of grace, I don't think it is any exaggeration to say that the general means of grace are something like the foundation upon which all the other means of grace ought to be built. If we think about the general means of grace as the right disposition of our hearts, then using the general means of grace denotes doing all the other means of grace with the right spiritual attitude and intention.

The Danger of Dissipation

The biggest pitfall we can fall into when we are practicing most of the means of grace is that we can start to do them in an unthinking way. Earlier, I simply said that these discipleship practices wouldn't be effective if we were just going through the motions when we were doing them. The consequences can actually be worse than that. And the reason is that it's not in our nature to just tread water in our spiritual lives. We're either sinking, or we're swimming.

There's a word to describe the danger we run into when we stop focusing on the inward disposition that we ought to have when we worship and pray and serve God. That word is "dissipation." Dissipation is what happens when water evaporates out of a boiling pot. It just vanishes into the air and goes away. Our love for God can dissipate like that when we are not actively working to remain centered on God. In a sermon on that subject, Wesley explains how significant a danger this can be:

We are encompassed on all sides with persons and things that tend to draw us from our center. Indeed, every creature, if we are not continually on our guard, will draw us from our Creator. The whole visible world, all we see, hear, or touch, all the objects either of our senses or understanding, have a tendency to dissipate our thoughts from the invisible world, and to distract our minds from attending to him who is both the author and end of our being.[4]

His biblical example for this experience is the story of Jesus in the home of Mary and Martha in Luke 10:38–42. Mary recognizes how important it is to sit and listen to the Lord of life when she has the chance, so she sits at his feet and soaks up his teaching. Martha, on the other hand, is distracted by household chores. Her faith is dissipated, even as the Son of God himself sits in her living room. She has become "unhinged from her proper center," as Wesley puts it elsewhere.[5]

Here is where the general means of grace become absolutely essential. They call us to stay focused on our proper center. To stay focused on God! We can be living outwardly good and dutiful lives—just as Martha was—but that doesn't mean we are connected to God at all. A living relationship with Jesus Christ will sanctify us. It will transform us by his holy love. One way of thinking about these general means of grace is that they show us the difference between simply doing good deeds and truly receiving God's gifts. If the right kind of inward intention is guiding our use of all the practices that make up the instituted and prudential means of grace, then we'll experience them not as deeds but as gifts of God for our salvation.

Impossible to Ignore:
Self-Denial and Cross-Bearing

In John Wesley's thinking, there are two of the general means of grace that especially explain the importance of our inward attitude because he thought they served as easy-to-understand examples: Jesus' twin commands to deny oneself and take up one's cross. About self-denial, Wesley says that "to deny ourselves is to deny our own will where it does not fall in with the will of God, and that however pleasing it may be."[6] When he talks about "our own will," the idea that he has in mind is that our own will is almost always going to lead us down the wrong path when left on its own. Because he often views the presence of sin as akin to a moral disease within us, Wesley tends to think of the effects of sin as constantly influencing toward thoughts, feelings, and actions that take us away from God. To deny ourselves would be to deny those basic worldly, sinful impulses that seem so attractive to us on their surface.

The flip side of the coin is Jesus' command to take up one's own cross. This has some real similarities to self-denial in the sense that cross-bearing also involves going against the natural tendencies we might have. Wesley writes, "A cross is anything contrary to our will, anything displeasing to our nature." While this is a companion to self-denial, it actually raises the bar in terms of what it requires of us. "[T]aking up our cross goes a little farther than denying ourselves," Wesley says, "it rises a little higher, and is a more difficult task to flesh and blood, it being easy to forego pleasure than to endure pain."[7] In other words, I can say "no" to something I would otherwise enjoy more easily than I can say "yes" to something that I positively don't want to do.

Why are these two ideas so important to Wesley's view of how our inward disposition is a general means of grace to us? Well, you can't really deny yourself the things you most want, or take up things that are truly difficult for you, without thinking about exactly why you are putting yourself through that kind of unpleasant process. You have to be intentional about it. You have to be focused on what it means to deny yourself, or to take up your cross in some specific way. There is no way to deprive yourself of one thing (or burden yourself with another) without your inward intention being at the center of that whole process.

We've looked a little bit at how our cultural mind-set of consumerism makes real discipleship difficult. (That was particularly the case in the chapter on fasting, which in some ways has a particularly strong connection with the general means of grace.) The world around us wants to encourage us to indulge ourselves and avoid things that are difficult. This is just the opposite of Jesus' commands to us! It may be that the general means of grace are needed now more than ever. We live lives of distraction: technology and media, in the form of smart phones and tablet computers and high-definition TVs, mean that we are rarely left alone with our thoughts. Contemplating ourselves and our relationship with God is so rare nowadays, in fact, that it is likely to make us fairly anxious when we first start to do it. I'm not sure there's anything more important though. Ultimately, we will never build the holy habit of patterning our lives according to the means of grace if we do not focus on the need for mindful attention in all that we are doing. In some ways, the general means of grace must be focused upon for all the other means of grace to make a difference.

Everywhere I have served as a pastor, one of the most common requests I get from church members when it comes to pastoral care is about how to navigate the difficulties of personal relationships. Sometimes this has to do with spouses and other family members. Sometimes it has to do with coworkers and friends. Whenever a church member of mine has presented me with a difficult situation, I would always ask how he or she had responded (or intended to respond). It almost never fails that people will give me an answer related to their level of comfort with personal interaction. Some would say they were going to send a text or an e-mail. Others would say they intended to pick up the phone and make a call. Very few people said they wanted to seek out the person with whom they had a disagreement, sit down together, and talk.

Now ask yourself this question: Why wouldn't the *first* reaction of people be to seek out those with whom things have become difficult so they could sit down together in person? I think it's probably all wrapped up with fear, anxiety, and the desire to avoid confrontation. My pastoral counsel to such folks is always to think about how they naturally wanted to respond and then move at least one level up on the difficulty scale. If the impulse was to send a text message, they ought to make a phone call. And if they naturally thought of making a phone call, they should instead seek the person out face-to-face. The goal, of course, would be to always seek out a person face-to-face, but not everyone can do that right off the bat.

In a small way, this is about denying oneself and taking up one's cross. Real relationships can be hard, but they are only built in a face-to-face manner. Doing the hard thing on the front end has positive consequences in the end. If you can think about your own discipleship like this, then you will begin to get a sense of how important the general means of grace are. We can use phrases that come from Jesus' mouth, like "obey the commandments," "deny yourself," and "take up your cross." Or, we can go with that little phrase that Wesley seemed to like so much: the exercise of the presence of God. The truth is that they are all pointing to the same idea, which is to be aware of God's presence in your life and live your life in response to the grace he gives you in every moment.

From Ordinary to Extraordinary

THERE ARE A COUPLE OF THINGS I HOPE YOU HAVE gained from reading this book. The first is that the Wesleyan vision for the means of grace offers a comprehensive framework for the spiritual life. People who have written on the means of grace in the past have recognized this fact very well. Hal Knight called it the "pattern of the Christian life."[1] Dean Blevins referred to the scope of the means of grace as an "ecology of holistic practices."[2] Ole Borgen referred to the total framework of the means of grace as the "environmental context" for Christian discipleship.[3] With each of those images, what is most dominant is the idea that the means of grace provide an

> The Wesleyan vision for the means of grace offers a comprehensive framework for the spiritual life.

entire model for living the Christian life in a way that leads to true spiritual growth. But note also what is required for that spiritual growth to happen: the means of grace must be embraced fully, with discipline, and within a community of fellow disciples.

Remember what I said back in the introduction about the three components essential for real discipleship? Those components are community, discipline, and transformation. We need a supportive and committed community of fellow disciples—a congregation, in other words—so that we can join together in the practice of our faith. We also need discipline, something a community is going to help out with quite a bit, but something which requires a deep personal commitment as well. (After all, no amount of encouragement from others will suffice if you aren't willing to embrace a disciplined faith yourself.) Beyond these two key elements of discipleship, the only "program" required is the means of grace themselves. They cover the range of practices that followers of Jesus are called to embrace.

The third component needed for authentic discipleship is the component of transformation. Transformation is God's work, rather than ours. But we will find God truly transforming our hearts and our lives when we engage in the means of grace with discipline and with a community of fellow Christians. Our use of the means of grace must be done with a searching and heartfelt faith, of course. No amount of mechanical going through the motions will do. All that faith requires, though, is the belief that we will find God in the means of grace. There is power in these practices, and the power is none other than that of the Holy Spirit.

The other thing I hope that reading this book has given you is a grasp of just how powerful the Wesleyan teaching on grace really is. John Wesley was a complicated and gifted person. He was a man of deep insight into the dynamics of the way of salvation—that journey from unbelief, to awakening, repentance, new birth, and growth in grace leading even unto perfection in love. Wesley was also a compelling writer of "practical divinity," the term he used for theology that was aimed at the practices of everyday Christians. He had remarkable gifts in organizing a complex movement of laity across both the British Isles and the North American colonies. And he had a profound desire throughout his entire adult life to engage in the work of renewal both for the national church to which he belonged and locally in countless villages, towns, and cities contained within the scope of his peripatetic work. Ultimately, Wesley's own personal spiritual journey is inseparable from all the other things he did. I think he understood both how difficult it is to "walk in the ways of God" in every way and how rewarding that calling can be when followed with perseverance.

> "Stir up the spark of grace which is now in you, and he will give you more grace."
>
> —John Wesley

At the heart of Wesley's spiritual teaching is, of course, the presence and power of God's grace. He believed that God's love for us is such that grace is always available to us, if we will but respond to it in faith. We all have a measure of that grace already, through Jesus Christ's willingness to come to us first when we know him not. It is that prevenient grace that allows Wesley to say with confidence, "Stir up the spark of grace which is now in you, and he will give you more grace."[4] The nature of grace is such that it never runs out. Unlike the finite resources of the world, the wonderful truth about grace is that the more we use it well, the more it will multiply and continue its redeeming work. "I do not give to you as the world gives," Jesus says in John 14:27 (NIV). No indeed, and the gift of love that Christ offers us is a gift both to transform us and to be shared with others in his name.

The means of grace can seem like such ordinary practices of discipleship, and indeed they are meant to be used in everyday, ordinary life. The promise that they hold for us is that they will show us the way from an ordinary to an extraordinary kind of life. How that happens is dependent upon God. It is true that we are called to be patient so that God's transforming work can happen in God's own good time. The counsel of Wesley for those impatient to see spiritual maturity take root in their own lives is simple. Transformation comes through the work of God's grace within us. Wesley teaches that all those who want to receive God's grace are called to "wait for it in the means which he hath ordained."[5] Those means are the means of grace, and together they provide us with all that we need for a life of true discipleship to Jesus Christ.

Discussion Starters

Introduction—Looking for Direction

1. How would you define a word like *discipleship*? What distinguishes a person who lives as a disciple of Jesus from other ways of life?

2. The way of discipleship calls for certain key things: rootedness in a faith *community*, the practice of *discipline* in the spiritual life, and the experience of personal *transformation*. The way of the world makes all of these things difficult, because of its tendency toward extreme *individualism*, rampant *consumerism*, and idolatrous *materialism*. What practical steps can you take to walk in the way of discipleship rather than the way of the world?

3. Are there any faith habits that you have developed in your own life that help you to "walk in the ways of God" each day? What originally drew you to them, and how did they develop in your life over time?

Chapter 1—What Does Grace Have to Do with Me?

1. Have you experienced God's grace as pardon for sins in your life? What was that like?

2. Have you encountered God's grace as power for healing in your life? When did that happen, and in what way were you healed?

3. There are two key New Testament words related to how God's grace works in our lives: *justification* and *sanctification*. In an important sense, our salvation

encompasses both of these. What questions did you have when you encountered these terms in this chapter?

Chapter 2—Baptism

1. Water plays a key role in the Bible in many different places. What are some of the Bible stories you know where water is featured prominently in some way?

2. Baptism is a sacrament in the Christian church. That means that something really *happens* at baptism. Which of the ways that baptism is a true means of grace made the most impact on you in this chapter?

3. Have you ever thought about your discipleship as learning to swim in the waters of your baptism? How does that image change the way you think about baptism generally?

Chapter 3—Searching the Scriptures

1. When we begin to grow familiar with the Scriptures, we grow closer to Jesus. Yet this same process can make us strangers to the world. What does it mean to you that searching the Scriptures might leave you dissatisfied with much of what you've come to assume about your life and the world around you?

2. John Wesley and many other Christian figures throughout history have taught that we will always find the Holy Spirit working in tandem with the teaching of Scripture. How does this thought suggest to us that searching the Scriptures could help us to encounter the power of God in a truly significant way?

3. Do you read the Bible regularly? If so, what approach do you use? If not, what do you think might help you to become a better student of the Scriptures?

Chapter 4—Prayer

1. Are there Bible passages about prayer that are important to you? Are these passages mostly stories (as when a biblical character is engaging in prayer), or are they actual prayers (like the Lord's Prayer or a psalm)? What makes them important to you?

2. One of the more arresting parts of John Wesley's teaching on prayer is that it is a kind of "spiritual respiration" between God and the Christian believer. What do you think he means by this?

3. What is your daily prayer life like? Are you satisfied with it, or would you like it to be different?

Chapter 5—The Lord's Supper

1. Have you ever thought about the connection between the Passover and the Lord's Supper in the Bible? What does it mean to you to think about the Lord's Supper as a sign of God's deliverance of us through Jesus Christ?

2. Have you ever had a profound spiritual experience while receiving Holy Communion? What was that like?

3. What is the practice of Holy Communion like in your church? How often is it celebrated? What kind of spiritual preparation do you undertake before receiving it?

Chapter 6—Fasting

1. Have you ever thought about how much fasting shows up in the Bible—both in the Old and New Testaments? Why don't we focus more on Scripture passages about fasting?

2. In Wesleyan teaching, we find fasting linked to other spiritual practices like prayer and the works of mercy. How might we take our spiritual lives more seriously if we incorporated fasting into them?

3. Do you fast? What is your practice of fasting like? Did you have a spiritual mentor who helped you understand how to fast, or did you develop the practice on your own?

Chapter 7—Fellowship

1. We think of ourselves as individuals. But the Bible always seems to assume that believers are united into a fellowship (like the church!). What difference does it make that the Scriptures seem almost always to be aimed at communities of people rather than individuals? Does that suggest anything about the relationship of Christian fellowship to the Christian faith itself?

2. One of the phrases that crops up in John Wesley's writing about the early Methodists is that they "watched over one another in love." What does it mean to watch over someone in love? Have other people ever watched over you in love?

3. Are you a part of a small group of other disciples that meets together on a regular basis? If so, what are your meetings like? Do you experience true spiritual growth in that setting?

Chapter 8—Classes, Bands, and Arts of Holy Living

1. The notion of "prudential means of grace" is one of the most fruitful parts of John Wesley's practical theology. Are there habits or practices in your own life that you have found to be true means of grace through the practical wisdom you've gained from life experience?

2. The General Rules were an important part of the foundation for discipleship in the early Methodist movement. Do you think a set of spiritual guidelines

like the General Rules would be helpful for the church today? Would such "arts of holy living" be helpful to you, personally?

3. Small groups like the class meetings and band meetings of the early Methodist movement are *particular* and *concrete* examples of Christian fellowship in action. Maybe they would work in our own context. And maybe not. What kind of small group structure do you think would be most effective today?

Chapter 9—Works of Mercy

1. One of the remarkable aspects of John Wesley's leadership was that he tried to embrace both biblical orthodoxy and missional flexibility. In other words, he believed that both the teaching of Scripture and the reality of contemporary life could be held together within the life of discipleship. What does that idea mean to you? How might it influence the way churches pursue their ministries?

2. The Scripture passage in Matthew 25:31–40 suggests to us that we will meet Jesus Christ when we engage in the works of mercy. What does this mean to you spiritually?

3. The works of mercy are more than just acts of charity toward the poor and sick. They are real *means of grace*, which means that they can be transformational for both those giving and those receiving the ministry. Have you ever found your life impacted by practicing the works of mercy?

Chapter 10—Exercising the Presence of God

1. When we practice the general means of grace, we find them always to bear fruit in our lives. The reason for

that is because the general means of grace cannot be done in a rote or unthinking manner. Given that, how can the general means of grace serve as the foundation for our practice of all the other means of grace?

2. There are ways in which specific practices can give shape to the general means of grace. One example would be fasting. It is one of the instituted means of grace, but it will always help us to experience the general means of grace that we call self-denial. Can you think of other specific practices that can help us experience self-denial, cross-bearing, the exercise of the presence of God, or some other general means of grace?

3. The general means of grace help to counter the danger of dissipation—that is, they keep our faith strong and vital. Have you thought about ways to embrace the general means of grace in your own life? What difference do you think that could make for your own discipleship?

Conclusion—From Ordinary to Extraordinary

1. At the beginning of this book, we looked at the way in which the three components of community, discipline, and transformation are essential to authentic Christian discipleship. Has reading this book made you think about how you can experience these things in greater ways in your daily life? In what ways?

2. Has your reading of this book caused you to think about the nature of God's grace in any new or fresh ways?

3. Do you have any thoughts about the way in which the means of grace can become the defining pattern of your own life?

Notes

Introduction: Looking for Direction

1. John Wesley, "The Late Work of God in North America," ¶I.7, in Volume 3 of *The Bicentennial Edition of the Works of John Wesley* (Nashville: Abingdon Press, 1976–), 59. Future references to this edition of Wesley's works will be cited as *Works of John Wesley*.

2. John Wesley, "Upon our Lord's Sermon on the Mount, XI," ¶III.6 in *Works of John Wesley* 1:674. Wesley's entire statement is worth quoting in full: "'Strive to enter in at the strait gate,' not only by this agony of soul, of conviction, of sorrow, of shame, of desire, of fear, of unceasing prayer, but likewise by 'ordering thy conversation aright,' by walking with all thy strength in all the ways of God, the way of innocence, of piety, and of mercy."

3. See, for example, Ann M. Graybiel and Kyle S. Smith, "Good Habits, Bad Habits," *Scientific American* (June 2014): 39–43.

4. The patterning language that I use in this chapter and in subsequent chapters has two sources. One is from Wesley himself. Wesley often employed such language when speaking about how we should look to exemplary Christians for models of how to pattern one's approach to the Christian life (e.g., "a pattern to the flock"). The other is more specifically about the means of grace serving as a pattern for the Christian life, which is an idea employed in various forms by Hal Knight in Henry H. Knight III, *The Presence of God in the Christian Life: John Wesley and the Means of Grace* (Metuchen, NJ: Scarecrow Press, 1992).

Chapter 1: What Does Grace Have to Do with Me?

1. John Wesley, *Instructions for Children* (Newcastle: John Gooding, 1746), 7.

2. A good example of Wesley's view of grace as the power of the Holy Spirit can be found in Wesley, "The Spirit of Bondage

and Adoption" (1746) [in *Works of John Wesley* 1:248–66].
The man under grace is described as one who has "the
power of the Holy Ghost, reigning in [his heart]" (¶III.1).
See similar statements in "The Good Steward" (1768)—"the
grace of God, the power of his Holy Spirit" (¶I.8.); and in
"The Means of Grace" (1746)—"the grace or power of the
Holy Ghost" (¶II.6).

3. The devotion I mention here was given by Bishop Gary E.
Mueller at the opening of the Extended Cabinet Retreat
of the Arkansas Conference UMC, First United Methodist
Church of Little Rock (September 16, 2014).

4. Vitale later said, "I honestly did not know how he was
going to make it up to the stage." See Dick Vitale,
"Jimmy V's legacy lives on," March 4, 2013, ESPN.
com. http://espn.go.com/espn/dickvitale/story/_/
id/9014571/20-years-famous-speech-jimmy-v-legacy-lives-on.

5. Jim Valvano, "ESPY Awards Speech," March 4, 1993. Online
at the website of The V Foundation for Cancer Research:
http://www.jimmyv.org/about-us/remembering-jim/jimmy
-v-espy-awards-speech/.

6. Wesley, "The Means of Grace," ¶II.1, in *Works of John Wesley*
1:381.

7. John Wesley highlights the passage from Acts 2:42–47 in
Wesley, "The Means of Grace," ¶I.1, in *Works of John Wesley*
1:378.

Chapter 2: Baptism

1. Jason Samenow, "Memphis flood: Mississippi river about to
crest," Capital Weather Gang Blog, *Washington Post* (May 9,
2011). Online at: http://www.washingtonpost.com/blogs
/capital-weather-gang/post/memphis-flood-mississippi-river
-about-to-crest/2011/05/09/AFpNj3ZG_blog.html.

2. Adrian Sainz, "$2.8B Damages in 2011 Mississippi River
Flood," *Associated Press* (February 25, 2013). http://bigstory
.ap.org/article/28b-damages-2011-mississippi-river-flood.

3. John Wesley, *Treatise on Baptism*, ¶I.1, in Albert C. Outler,
ed., *John Wesley* (New York: Oxford University Press, 1964),
319. All references to the *Treatise on Baptism* will come from
this edition. Only direct quotations will be cited by page
number.

4. Ibid.

5. John Wesley, "The Marks of the New Birth," ¶IV.2, in *Works of John Wesley* 1:428. I have taken slight liberties with this passage of Wesley's sermon to render it more accessible to the reader but have not changed the meaning that the passage intends to impart.

6. The great majority of Christians around the world affirm the baptism of infants and small children. But it is worth noting that there is also a small minority of Christians that deny the validity of infant baptism; they will go so far as to say that it is not baptism at all. People who hold this view will also cite Scripture passages to support their understanding of baptism, so that arguments about baptism can quickly turn into a game of "my verse trumps your verse." Here's a better way to think about the biblical support for infant baptism: we can and should employ the specific biblical texts that are, I believe, decisive for showing the truth of the Wesleyan view of baptism. And then we should also take care to ask the question: Just what do we think is happening at baptism? Is it just a testimony of faith received at some point in the past, an outward statement of what one already believes? If that's the case, then infant baptism really does run into problems. If baptism is a true *means of grace*, however, then we're talking about something different. It means we're talking about a gift of God, received by us through our worship where we are assured that God is present and at work.

7. I explain the context of Fred Edie's statement about learning to swim in our baptismal waters in Andrew C. Thompson, "Baptism, Youth Ministry, and the Means of Grace," *Liturgy* 29:1 (2014): 5–7.

Chapter 3: Searching the Scriptures

1. This passage is key to Wesley's view on how searching the Scriptures can be a true means of grace. See John Wesley, "The Means of Grace," ¶III.7, in *Works of John Wesley* 1:386–87.

2. See John Wesley, *Minutes of Several Conversations Between The Rev. Mr. Wesley and Others from the Year 1744, to the Year 1789*, commonly called the *Large Minutes*, in vol. VIII *The Works of John Wesley*, edited by Thomas Jackson, Reprint edition (Grand Rapids: Zondervan Publishing House, 1958), 322–24. Hereafter this edition of Wesley's works will be cited

as *Works of John Wesley (Jackson edition)*. Wesley's punctuation and capitalization in this section of the *Large Minutes* are strange and difficult for the reader, so I have corrected them for the sake of clarity. I have also switched the order of "hearing" and "meditating" for purposes of the explanation I offer in the paragraphs that follow.

3. Wesley, "The Means of Grace," ¶III.7, in *Works of John Wesley* 1:387.

4. John Wesley, *Journal* for June 26, 1740, in *Works of John Wesley* 19:158.

5. Wesley, "The Means of Grace," ¶II.3, in *Works of John Wesley* 1:382.

6. See Wesley, "The Means of Grace," ¶¶IV.1–2, in *Works of John Wesley* 1:390–91.

7. The resource I have personally used for many years is J. Ellsworth Kalas, *The Grand Sweep: 365 Days From Genesis Through Revelation* (Nashville: Abingdon Press, 1996). Dr. Kalas provides a very helpful schedule for reading, and his daily reflections never fail to shed light on the text for that day.

Chapter 4: Prayer

1. Arland J. Hultgren, "Prayer," in *The HarperCollins Bible Dictionary*, ed. Paul J. Achtemeier, et al. (New York: HarperCollins Publishers, 1996), 875.

2. "A Modern Affirmation," *The United Methodist Hymnal* (Nashville: The United Methodist Publishing House, 1989), 885.

3. John Wesley, "On Working Out Our Own Salvation," ¶II.4, in *Works of John Wesley* 3:205–6.

4. John Wesley, *A Plain Account of Christian Perfection*, Q.38.5 (Peterborough, UK: Epworth Press, 1952), 100.

5. Ibid., 101.

6. Ibid., 100–1.

7. Ibid., Q.38.8, 104.

8. John Wesley, "The New Birth," ¶II.4, in *Works of John Wesley* 2:193.

9. Clement of Alexandria, *Miscellanies*, Book VII, ¶39, translated by Fenton J. A. Hort and Joseph B. Mayor (London: MacMillan and Co., 1902), 69.

10. John Wesley, "Upon Our Lord's Sermon on the Mount, Discourse VI," ¶II.1, in *Works of John Wesley* 1:575.

11. Wesley, *Large Minutes*, Q.48, in *Works of John Wesley (Jackson edition)* 8:322.

12. John Wesley, "Upon Our Lord's Sermon on the Mount, VI," ¶II.1, in *Works of John Wesley* 1:575.

13. The basis for this prayer in Scripture can be found in Luke 18:13—the prayer of the tax collector in Jesus' parable of the Pharisee and the tax collector.

14. John Wesley, *A Plain Account of Christian Perfection*, Q.38.5, 101.

Chapter 5: Lord's Supper

1. John Wesley, "Upon Our Lord's Sermon on the Mount, VI," ¶III.11, in *Works of John Wesley* 1:584–585.

2. See John Wesley, "The Means of Grace," ¶III.11 and ¶II.1, in *Works of John Wesley* 1:389 and 1:381.

3. John Wesley, "The Duty of Constant Communion," ¶I.1, in *Works of John Wesley* 3:428.

4. Quoted passages in this paragraph are drawn from John Wesley, "The Duty of Constant Communion," ¶¶I.2–3, in *Works of John Wesley* 3:429.

5. John Wesley, "The Duty of Constant Communion," ¶¶I.2–3, in *Works of John Wesley* 3:429. Wesley's citation of 1 Corinthians 11:26 can be found in Wesley, "The Means of Grace," ¶III.11, in *Works of John Wesley* 1:389.

6. While the three-fold elements of memorial, means of grace, and sign of future glory are easily discernible in such Wesley texts as "The Duty of Constant Communion" and "The Means of Grace," I would be remiss if I did not mention that my reading of Wesley's sacramental theology is inseparable from my reading of the analyses of previous scholars such as Dean Blevins, Ole Borgen, Steve Harper, and Hal Knight. For two examples of earlier interpretations on this same topic, see Ole E. Borgen, "John Wesley: Sacramental Theology— No End without the Means," in *John Wesley: Contemporary Perspectives*, ed. John Stacey (London: Epworth Press, 1988), 69–81; and Steve Harper, *Devotional Life in the Wesleyan Tradition* (Nashville: Upper Room, 1983), 37–39.

7. Stanley Hauerwas, *In Good Company: The Church as Polis* (Notre Dame: University of Notre Dame Press, 1995), 48.

8. Wesley, "The Means of Grace," ¶III.12, in *Works of John Wesley* 1:389–90.

9. Charles Wesley, "O the Depth of Love Divine," *United Methodist Hymnal* (Nashville: United Methodist Publishing House, 1989), 627.

Chapter 6: Fasting

1. The prophet Samuel leads all of Israel in a fast of repentance, specifically to seek God's providential aid in battle against the Philistines (see 1 Samuel 7:3–11). Other examples include King Jehoshaphat in 2 Chronicles 20:3–12 and Ezra the priest in Ezra 8:21–23.

2. See Numbers 6:1–21.

3. See Judges 13:2–7 (for Samson) and 1 Samuel 1:9–11 (for Samuel). As most biblical commentators will point out, there were oddities about both Samson's and Samuel's Nazirite vows. One is that they were not voluntary, as was stipulated in Numbers. Both men were promised to God as Nazirites before they were even conceived! Another is that their vows were permanent: an angel visited Samson's mother and instructed her about the lifelong terms of Samson's vow; in the case of Samuel, his mother Hannah consecrated his life to God through prayer.

4. See Acts 18:18.

5. See, e.g., Luke 5:33–39 and Matthew 9:14–17.

6. John Wesley, "Upon our Lord's Sermon on the Mount, VII," ¶4, in *Works of John Wesley* 1:593.

7. John Wesley, *Large Minutes*, in *Works of John Wesley (Jackson edition)* 8:316–17.

8. Wesley, "Upon our Lord's Sermon on the Mount, VII," ¶IV.6, in *Works of John Wesley* 1:610.

9. See Matthew 6:5–18; Acts 13:2; and Acts 14:23.

10. Wesley's connection of fasting with Isaiah 58 comes specifically in "Upon our Lord's Sermon on the Mount, VII," ¶IV.7, in *Works of John Wesley* 1:610–11. While it is true that his favored biblical passage for discussing the works of mercy is from Matthew 25:31–41, in this instance he is connecting fasting with almsgiving in Matthew 6:2–4 (in the same way that he connects fasting with prayer from the same section of the Sermon on the Mount).

11. John Wesley, *Large Minutes*, in *Works of John Wesley (Jackson edition)* 8:316–17.

12. Tom Letchworth, "Self-control: Get a Grip!" Marion United Methodist Church (Marion, AR), September 7, 2014.

Chapter 7: Fellowship

1. My translator during this mission experience was Nic Poppe, who was at the time a student at Hendrix College in Conway,

Arkansas. I will always be grateful to Nic for his generous spirit and his willingness to facilitate my relationship with Pedro in its early days.

2. My use of "fellowship" may be confusing to some readers already familiar with Wesley's list of the instituted means of grace. Those who take their reading of Wesley's list from the version that appears in the later editions of the *Large Minutes* will typically insert "conference" as the final item. It is clear when Wesley's various lists of what he considers to be the instituted means of grace are compared (and when his uses of the term "fellowship" and "conference" themselves are compared) that the two terms are synonymous. For an example of fellowship within a lesser known listing of the instituted means, note this passage from Wesley's sermon, "Self-denial," where he lists the means of grace as consisting "of hearing the true word of God spoken with power; of the sacraments; or of Christian fellowship" (¶II.1, in *Works of John Wesley* 2:245).

3. John Wesley, *A Plain Account of the People called Methodists*, ¶I.11, in *Works of John Wesley* 9:259. What I call "false Christians" in brackets in this quote is termed by Wesley "devil Christians" in the original text. Wesley's original term—and the larger context in which it occurs in this treatise—would require a great deal more explanation, which is why I supply the synonym here.

4. Ibid.

5. John Wesley, *Journal* for March 25, 1780, in *Works of John Wesley* 23:162.

6. John Wesley, *A Plain Account of the People Called Methodists*, ¶II.7, in *Works of John Wesley* 9:262.

7. This statement might be offensive to some. After all, doesn't loving our neighbor mean loving everyone—regardless of creed? Isn't that what the parable of the Good Samaritan shows? Of course, I believe that loving one's neighbor means learning to love anyone with whom one comes into contact. Yet it's also true that such love has to begin somewhere. And if we are to learn how to love real people in a real way at all, we're likely to begin that process of transformation within the community of those that have a claim on our lives and to whom we belong. This I take to be the logic of Paul's statement in Galatians 6:10: "So then, as we have opportunity, let us do good to all men, and especially to those who are of the household of faith" (RSV).

Chapter 8: Classes, Bands, and Arts of Holy Living

1. For a helpful description of the role of context in discerning the prudential means of grace, see Dean Blevins, "The Means of Grace: Toward a Wesleyan Praxis of Spiritual Formation," *Wesleyan Theological Journal* 32:1 (Spring 1997): 79–80.

2. John Wesley, "Letter to the Revd. Samuel Wesley, Jun.," in *Works of John Wesley* 25:322. Wesley did not actually create the categories of "instituted" and "prudential" for the means of grace. He inherited those terms from an Anglican priest and theologian named John Norris who was a generation older than he. As with many of the things that became distinctive to Wesley's theology and the Methodist movement, though, his tendency was to take ideas or practices and develop them in creative and effective ways.

3. John Wesley, *The Nature, Design, and General Rules of the United Societies, in London, Bristol, Kingswood, and Newcastle upon Tyne* (Newcastle: John Gooding, 1743). I have taken minor liberties with the text and title of the General Rules, given otherwise distracting differences in spelling and punctuation.

4. John Wesley, *A Plain Account of Christian Perfection* (Peterborough: Epworth Press, 1952), 94.

5. The structure and purpose of the class meeting is described in David Lowes Watson, *The Early Methodist Class Meeting: Its Origins and Significance* (Nashville: Discipleship Resources, 1985), 94–97.

6. For a description of some of these organizational features of the band, see Kevin M. Watson, *Pursuing Social Holiness: The Band Meeting in Wesley's Thought and Popular Methodist Practice* (Oxford: Oxford University Press, 2014), 118–19 and 121–22.

7. John Wesley, *Journal* for April 4, 1739, in *Works of John Wesley* 19:47, speaking about the fruits experienced in band meetings.

8. Samuel Emerick, ed., *Spiritual Renewal for Methodism: There Is Redemptive Power in Personal Groups* (Nashville: Methodist Evangelistic Materials, 1958).

9. John Wesley, "Letter to Mrs. Susanna Wesley," in *Works of John Wesley* 25:283. His worry in this letter to his mother is about multiplying the prudential means of grace to such an extent that his focus on them would be counterproductive

and even distracting. Yet that very possibility shows how malleable and potentially fruitful the prudential means of grace can be.

10. The student was Bonnie Scott, and I don't know that I've ever heard a more apt description of the way grace works through spiritual disciplines.

Chapter 9: Works of Mercy

1. The quote is from Wesley, "On Visiting the Sick," ¶1, in *Works of John Wesley* 3:385. Wesley himself quotes the passage from Ephesians 2:10 in the same part of the sermon, although I have rendered it in the English Standard Version rather than the KJV to help readability.

2. John Wesley, *A Plain Account of the People Called Methodists*, ¶II.9, in *Works of John Wesley* 9:262–63.

3. Wesley, *A Plain Account of the People Called Methodists*, ¶II.11, in *Works of John Wesley* 9:263.

4. Both quotations in this paragraph are drawn from Wesley, *A Plain Account of the People Called Methodists*, ¶II.10, in *Works of John Wesley* 9:263.

5. The connection of the works of mercy with the love of neighbor is made most compellingly by Hal Knight in Knight, *The Presence of God in the Christian Life: John Wesley and the Means of Grace* (Metuchen, NJ: Scarecrow Press, 1992).

6. John Wesley, "Letter to Miss J. C. March, June 9, 1775," in vol. 6 of the *Letters of the Rev. John Wesley, A. M.*, edited by John Telford (London: Epworth Press, 1931), 153–54.

7. John Wesley, "On Visiting the Sick," ¶I.1, in *Works of John Wesley* 3:387.

8. In describing the consequences of failing to engage in the work of visitation, Wesley says, "If you do not, you lose a means of grace; you lose an excellent means of increasing your thankfulness to God, who saves you from this pain and sickness, and continues your health and strength; as well as of increasing your sympathy with the afflicted, your benevolence, and all social affections" ("On Visiting the Sick," ¶I.2, in *Works of John Wesley* 3:387).

9. John Wesley, "The Important Question," ¶III.5, in *Works of John Wesley* 3:191.

10. Rebekah Miles, "Works of Mercy as Spiritual Formation," in *The Wesleyan Tradition: A Paradigm for Renewal*, edited by Paul W. Chilcote (Nashville: Abingdon Press, 2002), 100.

Chapter 10: Exercising the Presence of God

1. The distinction between particular and general means of grace that I am making in this introductory section is made by Wesley himself in the minutes of the 1745 annual conference. See Albert C. Outler, ed., *John Wesley* (New York: Oxford University Press, 1964), 153.
2. John Wesley, *Large Minutes of 1780–89*, ¶48.7, in *Works of John Wesley* 10:924.
3. John Wesley, "Upon Our Lord's Sermon on the Mount, II," ¶II.3, in *Works of John Wesley* 1:496.
4. John Wesley, "On Dissipation," ¶6, in *Works of John Wesley* 3:118.
5. John Wesley, "The Important Question," ¶III.7, in *Works of John Wesley* 3:193.
6. John Wesley, "Self-denial," ¶I.6, in *Works of John Wesley* 2:243.
7. Ibid., ¶I.7, in *Works of John Wesley* 2:243.

Conclusion: From Ordinary to Extraordinary

1. As mentioned previously, the phrase, "pattern of the Christian life" and variants are used in Knight's *The Presence of God in the Christian Life: John Wesley and the Means of Grace* (Metuchen, NJ: Scarecrow Press, 1992).
2. See Dean Blevins, "The Means of Grace: Toward a Wesleyan Praxis of Spiritual Formation," *Wesleyan Theological Journal* 32:1 (Spring 1997): 71.
3. Borgen uses the phrase "environmental context" to refer specifically to the way in which all the means of grace are properly practiced within the framework of Christian conference in his major study of Wesley's sacramental theology. See Ole E. Borgen, *John Wesley on the Sacraments: A Definitive Study of John Wesley's Theology of Worship*, reprint edition (Grand Rapids: Francis Asbury Press, 1986), 119.
4. John Wesley, "On Working Out Our Own Salvation," ¶III.6 in *Works of John Wesley* 3:208.
5. John Wesley, "The Means of Grace," ¶III.1, in *Works of John Wesley* 1:384.